WORKING
with MEN'S
GROUPS
Roger Karsk & Bill Thomas

Volume

1

D1538673

WORKING
with MEN'S
GROUPS

Roger Karsk & Bill Thomas

Volume **Structured Exercises in:**

- **Consciousness Raising**
- **Self-Discovery**
- **Intimacy**
- **Parenting**

WHOLE PERSON ASSOCIATES
Duluth, Minnesota

Library of Congress Cataloging in Publication Data 87-50080
ISBN 0-938586-97-1

REPRODUCTION POLICY

*A portion of this material has been previously published under the same title in
1979 and 1987.*

Printed in the United States of America

10   9   8   7   6   5   4   3   2   1

WHOLE PERSON ASSOCIATES
210 West Michigan
Duluth MN 55802-1908
800-247-6789

To our Fathers, from where we started.

To our Brothers and Sisters, carrying on the struggle to enrich the present.

To Free Men in Columbia, Maryland, and elsewhere, spreading the vision of a new future.

CONTENTS

SEXUALITY AND INTIMACY

PARENTING

RESOURCES FOR MEN

PREFACE

It is hard to believe that fifteen years have passed since we first published this book. During that time, a great deal has changed about men's groups. Men have been celebrating their diversity and rediscovering or adopting once-abandoned traditions and rituals surrounding the male mystique. The 1980s found more men looking not to science but to literature and myth for their models, and writers such as Robert Bly reacquainted us with the depth of meaning available to us from those sources. As we approach a new century and men continue their search for self-discovery, the exercises we developed for the original version of this book have been updated and adapted to meet the needs of men in an ever-changing society.

Originally developed out of personal and professional experiences, this book helps leaders of men's groups focus their participants on the pains, joys, and confusion of being a man in today's society. As roles shift and change, many men find themselves without the anchors that once stabilized them. The exercises in this book do not provide new anchors. Instead, they serve as buoys—markers to help us chart a new course.

If the exercises allow men to strengthen themselves in their relationships, we will feel successful. If one man learns how to deal with his conflicts better, we will have made an impact. If one child and one father smile at each other more often, it will have been worthwhile.

This book is also the result of many hours of work in a little office in Columbia, Maryland, with four white walls and mountains of paper. Those hours nurtured dialogues that provided valuable insights, and many of those discoveries have found their way into this book. That office served as a meeting ground for us to integrate our ideas with those of others.

Among those others, the following deserve special mention: Glen Gaumnitz, Ed Dworkin, Charlie Murphy, Marc Young, Rick Rutherford, Dick Franklin, Donna Rose, Mike Nord, Howard and Rae Millman, Steve Landsman, Dick Conoboy, and Gene Martin. Other members of Free Men assisted with support of time, ideas, and resources. To those mentioned and many others, especially those who had to put up with our absence (or presence) while we worked on developing and revising the book, thanks!

Roger Karsk and Bill Thomas
Baltimore, Maryland, 1994

INTRODUCTION

Working with Men's Groups has been developed as a tool for those who lead groups of men. Each exercise, while involving diverse activities surrounding a variety of issues, follows a structured pattern to provide trainers with step-by-step instructions for creating successful workshops. (For a complete explanation on how the exercises work as well as some valuable information on instructing groups, please read "How to Use This Book Most Effectively" in the Resources section.) The exercises are divided into four sections covering the central issues focused on by most of today's men's groups: Self-Discovery, Consciousness Raising, Sexuality and Intimacy, and Parenting.

The exercises in the Self-Discovery section reflect the past three decade's increase in the number of men who take the time for introspection. They provide participants with an opportunity to look within to help themselves discover the true source of their problems and take steps to change them. They also create a situation where men spend time with others who share similar ideas and experiences—other men with fears and anxieties like their own—which often helps participants break out of isolation and liberate themselves from carrying their burdens alone.

While Self-Discovery helps participants discover themselves as individuals, the Consciousness Raising section asks participants to examine themselves from the perspective of being male. Based on the once-a-week format of traditional gender role consciousness raising groups, the exercises in this section provide participants with an opportunity to develop positive, healthy relationships with other men, experience the kind of impact and energy unique to an all-male group, get in touch with their anger, validate their feelings, explore alternative behaviors, and discover new role models.

As men become self-aware and their consciousness is raised, they become more in touch with their own feelings and those of others. This reconnection, which often affects their attitudes toward sexual relations and intimacy, prompted us to develop the exercises in the Sexuality and Intimacy section. The exercises help the leader guide men to a greater understanding of their own sexuality and that of their partners, define a clear difference between being intimate and being sexual, and recognize sexual harassment and develop strategies to change inappropriate behavior in themselves and others.

While the exercises in the Sexuality and Intimacy section help men become better friends and partners with their significant others, those in the Parenting section will help them become better fathers to their children. Since few people successfully alter their behavior until they understand its origin, the exercises are designed to provide participants with a greater understanding of how they parent and their feelings connected to parenting and to how they themselves were raised. Specifically, they examine how men parent, society's expectations of fathers, and some basic dilemmas fathers encounter through various stages of parenthood.

Society, in its struggle to make up for the inequities of the past, has often devalued traditional power groups in order to elevate groups of people who have been treated unfairly. The concerns of women are currently being addressed—a very positive step, but one that has unfortunately caused men as a whole to be seen in an unflattering light. Instead of continuing to address the wrongs men have committed over the centuries, we must focus on eliminating misconceptions and raising awareness of our behaviors—good and bad—in order to direct our energies to becoming better, well-rounded individuals. The exercises in this book strive to help men do just that.

Self-Discovery

SELF-DISCOVERY

Despite Plato's command to "Know thyself," most men spend the bulk of their time and energy looking outward. They pay attention to objects and activities around them—work, family, possessions. Part of this may come from education and upbringing, from systems that reward doing and not being—systems that push us to work together yet teach us to keep our feelings and innermost thoughts to ourselves.

One by-product of the human growth movements of the past three decades is an increase in the number of men who have taken the time for introspection. What they have found has sometimes been unpleasant, has often surprised them, and has even offered liberation.

Because of everyday pressures, most men usually do not take time to look within. Sooner or later, however, their bodies or behaviors indicate something is wrong. The roots of the problem may lie in dissatisfaction, feelings of inadequacy, pressures in the work world, or responsibilities and relationships in a family. Most men assume their pressures come from outside, underestimating how much pressure they put on themselves. Looking within can help them discover the true problem and take steps to change it.

Examining these pressures, however, can be risky business. One may discover parts of himself he finds difficult to deal with—"embarrassing" feelings and attitudes that cry out for a major life change. In a non-supportive setting, these discoveries often overwhelm the individual.

The exercises in this section assist men as they open windows on themselves. Do not push your participants beyond levels they can deal with—group members participate according to their personal comfort level. The strength of these exercises comes from bringing men together—asking them to set aside cocktail glasses, work, talk of sports or the market—to share some of their emotions and thoughts. Many participants find spending time with others who share similar ideas and experiences very liberating. Realizing that other men have fears and anxieties like their own helps some men break out of isolation.

These exercises focus on the past, present, and future, and most aim toward a heterogeneous grouping of men, so your participants will be richer for that variety. They can be used in a variety of ways—singly, as part of an ongoing series, or in a full day (or longer) workshop. The possible combinations are many, but keep in mind that Exercise 1, "Who Am I As A Man?" and Exercise 2, "Who Is That In The Mirror?" serve best as introductory exercises since their general nature begins to focus participants inward. Exercise 3, "Crazy Ideas," and Exercise 4, "Imaginary Dialogues," invite participants to probe further, so they make excellent follow-up exercises.

Exercise 5, "Like You/Unlike You," requires that some degree of trust already exists in the group. It serves to deepen members' understanding of each other and should be implemented after the introductory exercises mentioned above. Participants take this exercise as far as they are prepared to go, so the group leader needs to know his own level of comfort in order to maintain control of the exercise. This design may be preceded or followed by Exercise 6, "Through Others' Eyes," which provides an opportunity for participants to explore the way others feel about them and also assumes that some degree of trust exists in the group. The trainer needs to be sensitive to the trust issue especially when working with a large group, so that some participants do not delve deeper than others are willing to go.

Exercise 7, "The Role Crunch;" Exercise 8, "Yours, Mine, and Ours;" Exercise 9, "Wholly Man/Holy Man;" Exercise 10, "Same Yet Different;" Exercise 11, "Single Man;" and Exercise 12, "Facing Retirement;" deal with specific categories or roles and, obviously, won't be important to all members of your groups. They should, in any case, come after the initial six general exercises have prepared participants for introspection and sharing.

Finally, Exercise 13, "Give Yourself Strokes," provides an excellent way to end a workshop. It is nonthreatening and creates a great deal of positive feedback.

1 WHO AM I AS A MAN?

In this introductory exercise, participants get to know themselves and one another by completing open-ended sentences and discovering, examining, and sharing their personal set of values.

GOALS

To allow group members an opportunity to get acquainted.

To examine personal values.

To share those values with others.

TIME

1 hour.

GROUP SIZE

6–24 participants.

MATERIALS

Newsprint; markers; pens or pencils; **My Values** worksheets.

PROCESS

☞ *Since this exercise works as an introductory activity, you may wish to begin by welcoming participants and outlining the exercises and activities you have planned for the session.*

1. Introduce the exercise and its goals with a chalktalk based on the following statements:

   • We all have our own personal set of values, our own "list" of what is important to us.

   • Most of us, however, don't consciously think about these values; rather, we display them through what we say and do.

   • Today we are going to take the time to examine some of our values and then discuss them with each other.

2. Distribute the **My Values** worksheet and allow participants fifteen minutes to complete the open-ended sentences.

3. When the participants have completed the worksheet, ask them to select a partner and spend five minutes each discussing their answers.

4. Have pairs combine with two other pairs (forming groups of six) and discuss what they found to be helpful or difficult when completing the worksheet and share any discoveries they made about themselves.

5. After about twenty minutes, reconvene the entire group and select one person from each small group to summarize the most important insights they have gained.

   ☞ *Record the responses on newsprint.*

6. Summarize the major issues raised by the entire group and end with closing comments based on the following:

   - This exercise has shown us that as men, we all share common values and concerns.

   - Until today, however, many of you may not have realized that other men thought about these issues the same way you do.

   - We have discovered that we can use each other as sounding boards— as tools to help each other work out the conflicts large or small that we encounter every day.

VARIATIONS

   ■ In place of *Steps 4* and *5*, you could reconvene the entire group and have each person share his responses to particular open-ended sentences, initiating a group discussion based on common replies.

   ■ If you are using this exercise to initiate an ongoing group or workshop, use *Step 6* to explain how the issues raised during this exercise will be addressed in future activities.

MY VALUES

1. As a man, I am . . .

2. As a man, I think . . .

3. As a man, I feel . . .

4. As a man, I assume . . .

5. As a man, I would like to be . . .

6. As a man, I hate . . .

7. To me, men are . . .

8. The thing I like most about me is . . .

9. The thing I like most about men is . . .

10. The thing I like most about women is . . .

11. The thing I like least about me is . . .

12. The thing I like least about men is . . .

13. The thing I like least about women is . . .

14. The most important thing in a relationship is . . .

15. Intimacy with a man differs from intimacy with a woman because . . .

16. My work is . . .

17. My family is . . .

18. My friends are . . .

©1995 Whole Person Press 210 W Michigan Duluth MN 55802   (800) 247-6789

2 WHO IS THAT IN THE MIRROR?

This introspective introductory activity examines life-styles and the effects of the way we treat ourselves physically. Makes an excellent follow-up or alternative to Exercise 1.

GOALS

To become more aware of how we treat our own bodies.

To become more sensitive to our life-style and its effect on us.

TIME

1 hour.

GROUP SIZE

6–24 participants.

MATERIALS

Newsprint; markers; pens or pencils; **Life-style Questionnaire** worksheets.

PROCESS

1. Introduce the exercise and its goals with a chalktalk based on the following statements:

   • Many popular magazine articles and television "news magazine" stories deal with trends concerning "life-styles."

   • Our life-style is simply what we do on an average day—what we eat and drink, our work habits, and the physical activities we participate in—basically, how we treat ourselves.

   • Some people are very aware of their life-style, watching what they eat and exercising regularly; others may not have ever stopped to think about the way they live.

   • Today we will examine our life-styles in order to become more aware of how we treat our bodies and, therefore, ourselves.

2. Distribute the **Life-style Questionnaire** worksheets and allow participants about fifteen minutes to complete them.

3. When participants have finished, form small groups and have them spend ten minutes discussing their immediate reactions to the worksheet questions.

4. Have participants remain in their small groups and allow sufficient time for those who wish to individually report the answers on their worksheets and receive feedback from the others.

5. Reconvene the entire group and select one person from each small group to summarize the most important lesson they have learned.

   ☞ *Record the responses on newsprint.*

6. Summarize the major issues raised by the entire group and generate a closing discussion with the following questions:

   ✔ How many of you are completely satisfied with your life-style?

   ✔ How many think you need to change some of your behaviors?

   ☞ *Ask for a show of hands. The overwhelming majority of your participants will probably respond to the second question.*

   ✔ What steps can you take to change that behavior—to create a more positive, healthy life-style for yourself?

   ☞ *Some common responses may include joining a health club or exercise class, starting a diet program, quitting bad habits, etc. Suggest some organizations or services in your area for those participants who express serious interest in changing their life-style.*

VARIATIONS

■ In place of *Step 4,* select several specific items from the worksheet and have all members of each group discuss their answers. Then in *Step 5,* have each group report their responses, list them on newsprint, and generate a discussion by asking questions about common or opposing replies.

LIFE-STYLE QUESTIONNAIRE

1. What is your weight? How does it compare to five years ago? What should it be?

2. What is your cholesterol count? Your blood pressure? When was the last time you had these tested?

3. When was the last time you looked in the mirror and really assessed how you looked? What do you look for? What do you notice first when you look in a mirror?

4. Have you ever seen a recent photograph of yourself and did not believe that it was you? If so, why?

5. What did you eat and drink yesterday? (List everything.) Is it balanced? Does it include salads? How much sugar? Coffee?

   Do you typically eat 6 meals each day:
   BREAKFAST   snacks   LUNCH   snacks   DINNER   snacks?

6. Do you take any vitamins? What? How much? When?

7. How much sleep do you get every night? Is it restful or do you toss and turn? Do you take naps?

LIFE-STYLE QUESTIONNAIRE, continued

8. How many hours a day do you work? How often do you take work home at night? On weekends? Do you use up your vacation days?

9. How much alcohol do you drink per week? How do you feel about this? When was the last time you went out socially with another man and did not have a drink?

    Below list the number of drinks you had during the last week:

    | Monday | ___ | Thursday | ___ | Saturday | ___ |
    | Tuesday | ___ | Friday | ___ | Sunday | ___ |
    | Wednesday | ___ | | | | |

10. How much do you exercise per week? Do you jog? Do you walk each day? Do you play tennis? Do you swim?

11. How much television do you watch per week?

12. How is your sex life? How often do you have sex? Are you satisfied when you do? Do you avoid it? What do you look for most in a sex partner? What do you notice first?

13. What do you want to change?

©1995 Whole Person Press 210 W Michigan Duluth MN 55802   (800) 247-6789

3 CRAZY IDEAS

By listing some of the myths they learned as children, participants examine
how the internalization of some ideas has resulted in their preconceptions
about certain activities and groups.

GOALS

To understand the influences on our development as exemplified by ideas
we have internalized.

To appreciate the effects of those ideas on our growth and behavior.

To identify ways we transmit similar ideas.

TIME

1 hour.

GROUP SIZE

6–24 participants.

MATERIALS

Newsprint; markers; tape; pens or pencils; **Where Did I Get These Crazy
Ideas?** worksheet.

PROCESS

1. Introduce the exercise and its goals and use the following question to
   draw participants into the activity:

   ✔ Recall when you were young: what crazy ideas—particularly,
   reasons for doing or not doing something—did you learn from
   others?

   ☞ *Invite them to share aloud. You can break the ice with an
   example such as, "You'll go blind from masturbating." If you
   receive mostly humorous comments, identify other, more
   serious categories (e.g., race, religion, hygiene, etc.)*

2. Distribute the worksheet and allow ten minutes for participants to fill
   it out.

3. Form small groups of three or four and have participants spend ten
   minutes sharing their responses, comparing and contrasting them.

©1995 Whole Person Press 210 W Michigan Duluth MN 55802   (800) 247-6789

4. Have the small groups examine the positive and negative effects these ideas have or had on behavior (i.e., What did the ideas free the participants to do? What did it keep them from doing?).

5. Reconvene the entire group and ask participants to share representative examples and comments.

    ☞ *Record the responses on newsprint.*

6. Summarize the common responses and generate a closing discussion with the following questions:

    ✔ Why do you suppose our "teachers" in life told us these wild ideas?

        ☞ *Most responses will suggest that the sources of the information were either being protective or were themselves misinformed.*

    ✔ Even if some of the ideas were taught "for our own good," have they harmed us in any ways?

    ✔ Do we transmit misconceptions to the children in our lives? How?

    ✔ Should we continue to proliferate some of these misconceptions to the young people around us?

WHERE DID I GET THESE CRAZY IDEAS?

Directions: In the spaces below, list some crazy ideas you learned while growing up and identify who taught you the idea by checking the appropriate box on the right (P = Parents, R = Relatives, T = Teachers, F = Friends).

MY CRAZY IDEAS	P	R	T	F

4 IMAGINARY DIALOGUES

Using each other as a sounding board, participants reduce anxiety by speaking aloud what they would like to say to someone important to them.

GOALS

To identify those to whom we feel we have something important to say.

To fashion a way to say what we need to say.

TIME

1–1½ hours.

GROUP SIZE

8–12 participants.

MATERIALS

None.

PROCESS

1. Introduce the exercise and its goals with a chalktalk based on the following statements and rhetorical questions:

   • Have you ever put off saying something important to someone you care for because you're afraid of their reaction?

   • Is there something important you need to say to someone with whom it is impossible to speak? Someone who has died, for instance?

   • Whether you are delaying a conversation or find it impossible to have one, it is still important to say what you feel you need to say— to get things off your chest.

   • This exercise, which is primarily personal, will allow us an opportunity to practice what we would like to say to someone or to say something to someone we cannot contact.

2. Provide the following instructions:

   ➤ Think of one or two significant people in your life to whom you have something important to say. They may be living or dead, prominent now or in the past. They may be family members or friends or even people you haven't met but who have influenced you in some way.

➤ Choose one of those people and imagine what you would want to say to him or her if he or she were in this room.

3. After several minutes, instruct participants to pair up with someone they trust and spread themselves throughout the room.

☞ *If space allows, pairs should be far enough apart so that their dialogues do not disturb others.*

4. Give the pairs the following instructions:

➤ One person should address the other as if he were the person to whom the first needs to speak. Say everything to your partner you would like to say to the important person in your life.

➤ The partner listening should not respond when spoken to, even if the speaker asks questions.

➤ After fifteen minutes, I will call time and you will switch roles, allowing the other to speak.

➤ Do not discuss your dialogues at this time; you will have a chance to describe the experience later in the exercise.

➤ Speakers can practice as many times as they wish or address as many people as they like.

☞ *Circulate around the room and pay attention to the reactions of each speaker so you can better respond to them in the discussion generated in Step 5.*

5. After everyone has had a chance to speak, reconvene the entire group and use the following questions to generate a closing discussion:

✔ What feelings did you experience while you spoke?

✔ What feelings did you experience while you listened?

✔ What did you learn about yourself during this exercise?

6. Ask participants whether they are "finished" with their dialogue or need to say more, and if so, whether they need to address that person directly. If so (and if time allows) provide an opportunity for those who wish to continue their dialogue or to rehearse it with other group members.

VARIATIONS

■ If your group is small and their trust level is high, individuals can practice their dialogues in front of the entire group. This usually generates more feelings in the listeners. Do not use this variation if there is only one facilitator, since one person may not be able to handle the dynamics of the person in the middle as well as those of the men around the circle.

5 LIKE YOU / UNLIKE YOU

To define their individuality within a group and recognize the individuality of others, participants compare themselves to one another and discuss their similarities and differences.

GOALS

To explore how we are similar to others yet unique individuals at the same time.

TIME

1–1½ hours.

GROUP SIZE

6–24 participants.

MATERIALS

Newsprint; markers; tape.

PROCESS

1. Introduce the exercise and its goals with a chalktalk based on the following statements and rhetorical questions:

   • Take a look at your fellow group members. How are they like you? (Besides gender!) Do they all look the same? Dress the same? Do they look and dress like you?

   • You probably think that many of your colleagues look and dress the same as each other, but not like you.

   • While we all belong to many groups—gender, racial, religious, political, etc.—we still think of ourselves as individuals.

   • During this exercise, we will take stock of ourselves and each other to identify how we are all very different and still very much the same.

2. Have participants form pairs with someone they trust.

3. Instruct the pairs to look at each other and take turns completing the following sentence:

   • We both have _____, but mine is (are) _____ and yours is (are) _____.

©1995 Whole Person Press 210 W Michigan Duluth MN 55802   (800) 247-6789

4. After about six rounds of "We both have . . . ," (about ten minutes) instruct participants to spend the next fifteen minutes discussing several particular aspects of their lives (work, hobbies, sports, etc.), focusing on each person's involvement in that area and comparing their similarities and differences.

5. Ask pairs to combine, forming small groups of four, and have individuals take turns introducing their partners, focusing on what they learned about one another during *Step 4*.

6. After each has finished (about twenty minutes) reconvene the entire group and initiate a discussion using the following questions:

   ✔ How many people were surprised by what they discovered about their fellow group members?

   ✔ Was anyone surprised at what they have in common with other group members? Pleasantly?

   ✔ Have you ever cut yourself off from others because they're like you or unlike you? Why?

7. Close the activity by asking each participant to identify something new he learned about himself.

VARIATION

■ Another way to close this activity would be to show Rosabeth Moss Kanter's videotape **Tale of O** and compare the dynamics of difference it describes with what was discussed in the activity. You could also use the tape in a particularly homogeneous group (e.g., middle-aged white males) to segue into an exploration of how they treat others who are not members of their own affinity group. This is a good way for a predominately homogeneous group to begin to deal with issues of diversity.

Tale of O is available in both 18 and 27 minute versions for $695.00 from Good Measures Inc., 1 Memorial Drive, Cambridge, MA 02142 or by calling 1-800-969-0779.

6 THROUGH OTHERS' EYES

Participants use role playing to examine how they think others perceive them and how those beliefs and feelings affect their actions.

GOALS

To understand our assumptions about, and perceptions of, others' attitudes or feelings toward us.

To understand our actions and reactions based on these assumptions.

TIME

1 1/2–2 hours.

GROUP SIZE

6, 9, or 12 participants for each facilitator.

MATERIALS

Newsprint; markers; tape; pens or pencils; writing paper.

PROCESS

1. Introduce the exercise and its goals and give the following instructions:

   ➤ Take a few minutes to consider a relationship with someone significant in your life— a friend, spouse, parent, child, coworker, etc.— that you would like to explore today.

2. Divide the group into trios, identifying each member as either "A," "B," or "C," and give the following instructions:

   ➤ A should describe to B the significant person he chose to explore (and their relationship) while C observes, noting significant comments.

   ➤ You will then engage in a role play: A plays his significant other and B plays A. During your role play, discuss an issue important to that relationship, one you have explained to your role playing partner.

   ➤ While A and B are role playing, C should observe, noting moments of high energy, feelings, and behaviors that draw reactions from A.

   ➤ When I call time, you will have thirty seconds to end the role play.

☞ *If participants appear to be puzzled by these somewhat complex instructions, ask for two volunteers to demonstrate the process with you.*

3. After ten minutes, call time. Allow the trios thirty seconds to end their role play, then give the following directions:

   ➤ With C recording, A and B are to list what they are currently feeling and what they felt during the role play.

   ➤ Next, C should relate his observations to A and B.

   ➤ Finally, focusing on A, the trios use the following questions to discuss what they learned:

      ✔ Did A find anything significant in B's portrayal of him?

      ✔ Did A learn anything about himself and his significant other?

      ✔ Did B or C notice any behaviors in A that were inconsistent with his description of the relationship they explored?

4. Repeat *Steps 2, 3*, and *4*, this time switching roles: B plays his significant other, C plays B, and A observes.

5. Repeat *Steps 2, 3*, and *4* again, switching roles once more: C plays his significant other, A plays C, and B observes.

6. Reconvene the entire group and have each trio report significant discoveries they made during the role play.

7. Close with a chalktalk focusing on how assumptions and perceptions affect relationships:

   ● We all have our own perceptions about how the people in our lives think and feel about us.

   ● As we have seen today, while we don't always consciously consider it, these perceptions color the way we act and react when we are with or thinking about those people.

   ● Understanding these perceptions can help us understand how the people in our lives help shape who we are.

   ● For example. . . .

      ☞ *Using your participants' comments as examples, clarify points and complete your chalktalk.*

VARIATIONS

■ If this exercise is used in a couples' workshop, couples can reverse roles. Keep in mind how powerful gender reversal can be and pay special attention to participants for whom the experience may become overwhelming.

■ A short discussion of the Johari Window, which explores the dynamics of self-disclosure and feedback, makes an appropriate short lecture to complete the activity. One presentation of this theory appears in Lawrence Porter's *Reading Book for Human Relations Training*. (see the Self-Discovery Reading List on pages 41 and 42)

©1995 Whole Person Press 210 W Michigan Duluth MN 55802   (800) 247-6789

7 THE ROLE CRUNCH

Designed for participants currently involved in a domestic partnership, this exercise explores the different roles partners play and their effect on relationships.

GOALS

To look at how we divide household roles.

To examine how we see our role in respect to traditional household tasks.

TIME

1–1 1/2 hours.

GROUP SIZE

6–24 participants.

MATERIALS

Newsprint; markers; pens or pencils; **Responsibility Chart** worksheets.

PROCESS

1. Introduce the exercise and its goals with a chalktalk based on the following statements:

   - Not too long ago, the vast majority of couples played "traditional" roles, with one partner working as the wage earner while the other worked as homemaker.

   - Today, of course, both partners in most couples work, placing those traditional roles under scrutiny.

   - We now question how household responsibilities should be shared when both partners work full time or when one partner works full time and the other works part time or does not work outside the home. When one partner takes a full-time job, should the other be expected to take on more responsibilities at home?

   - Today we will examine how we divide traditional household roles with our partners.

2. Have each participant select a definition from the list below that most accurately describes their partnership:

☞ *Write these on newsprint prior to exercise.*

➤ **Helping:** I help my partner in some areas.

➤ **Shared:** We have worked out a system in which we equally share the responsibilities of the house and kids.

➤ **Traditional:** I am the bread winner, my partner is the homemaker.

➤ **Responsible:** I take responsibility for the house and kids and my partner helps me.

3. Define the terms "**Shared-Responsibility Role Crunch**" and "**Shared-Finances Role Crunch**."

    ☞ *Write these on newsprint so participants can refer to them.*

    • A **Shared-Responsibility Role Crunch** occurs when the breadwinner takes on added responsibility at home, yet the homemaker still does not contribute to the family finances.

    • A **Shared-Finances Role Crunch**, occurs when the homemaker returns to work outside the house, but the breadwinner still expects the homemaker to handle all the responsibilities of the house and kids.

4. Form groups of six and provide the following instructions:

    ➤ Take turns briefly explaining which definition you selected and why.

    ➤ Discuss both role crunches using the following questions:

        ✔ Has anyone in the group ever experienced either role crunch?

        ✔ What was it like?

        ✔ What did you do to overcome the problems it created?

5. After fifteen minutes, distribute the **Responsibility Chart** worksheets and give participants ten minutes to complete it.

6. Have the small groups spend approximately thirty minutes discussing their responses, specifically, their feelings about their answers, if their responsibilities have changed, and if they need additional changes.

    ☞ *Depending on the makeup of the group, significant life changes (retirement, a new marriage, etc.) and their effects on roles and responsibilities could be addressed. Stress that not everyone will have or will be comfortable with the same arrangement, and the goal of the activity is not to get anyone to change unwillingly.*

7. Reconvene the entire group and close the session by asking for a show of hands of those who felt they needed additional changes, then have the group members help each other by brainstorming ideas for initiating those changes.

RESPONSIBILITY CHART

Directions: Using a check mark, indicate under the columns on the right who now is responsible for each of the areas listed on the left:

	Me	Partner	Equal	Comments
Earning Income				
Cooking				
Cleaning House				
Dishes				
Laundry				
Grocery Shopping				
Finances (budget, bill paying)				
Investments				
Major Decisions: a. Buying a house b. Buying a new car c. Stock investment				
Car Maintenance				
Children: a. Transportation b. Clothes shopping c. Doctor & dentist appointments d. Recreation e. Staying home when they are ill				
Lawn Maintenance				
House Maintenance				
Pets				
Other				

©1995 Whole Person Press 210 W Michigan Duluth MN 55802   (800) 247-6789

8 YOURS, MINE, AND OURS

Participants explore their perceptions about personal property and clarify how they share expenses with their partner as a way to consider whether their current system is satisfactory.

GOALS

To clarify our perceptions of what property belongs to whom.

To clarify how our incomes are divided.

TIME

1 1/2–2 hours.

GROUP SIZE

6–24 participants.

MATERIALS

Newsprint; markers; pens or pencils; **Our Stuff** worksheets.

PROCESS

☞ *This design works well in conjunction with Exercise 7,* **The Role Crunch.**

1. Introduce the exercise and its goals with a chalktalk based on the following statements:

    • In a time when both partners in the majority of couples work, it becomes increasingly important to be very specific about how property is divided and whose income is used to pay which bills.

    • Often, for example, one person will continue paying most of the major bills even when both partners work.

    • This activity will give us an opportunity to clarify how we perceive our "ownership" of both possessions and financial responsibilities.

2. Distribute the worksheets and allow about fifteen minutes for participants to complete them.

3. Form small groups and have participants spend about thirty minutes sharing answers to **Section 1** of the worksheet.

4. Have the groups share their responses to **Section 2**: What their present system is? How satisfied they are with it (their rating)? What they want to change about it?

5. Reconvene the entire group and close by listing the different systems used by participants so they can plan changes they may want to make in their own; allow participants to ask questions.

☞ *Responses typically cluster in three or four systems.*

VARIATION

■ This design could easily be used with couples with only slight modifications:

a. Allow more time for couples to explore their lists, their differing perceptions, and their level of satisfaction.

b. Lead them into action planning about those parts of their arrangement they are dissatisfied with.

OUR STUFF, part 1

WHAT'S MINE, WHAT'S YOURS, WHAT'S OURS

Directions: List in the appropriate column the possessions that belong to you, your partner, or both of you. If you think your partner would disagree, place a check in the column on the right.

Mine	My Partner's	Ours	✓

How do you as a couple decide which category a new item goes into? Do you have a system? Explain it briefly.

OUR STUFF, part 2

WHO PAYS FOR WHAT?

Directions: Write a brief description of how you and your partner divide your total income to pay basic bills such as housing, food, medical expenses, etc.

Circle the number below that best indicates how satisfied you are with the arrangement you described above.

LEVEL OF SATISFACTION

Low   1   2   3   4   5   6   7   8   9   10   **High**

What aspect(s) of your present system would you like to change?

©1995 Whole Person Press 210 W Michigan Duluth MN 55802   (800) 247-6789

9 WHOLLY MAN / HOLY MAN

This introspective exercise provides participants with an opportunity to explore their own spirituality and the role spirituality plays in their lives.

GOALS

To understand our own definitions of spirituality.

To explore our feelings about being "spiritual" men.

To understand the role spirituality plays in our lives.

TIME

2 hours.

GROUP SIZE

6–18 participants.

MATERIALS

Newsprint; markers; tape; colored pencils; crayons.

PROCESS

1. Introduce the exercise by asking the following questions:

   ✔ How many of you consider yourselves spiritual?

   ✔ What exactly is spirituality?

   ☞ *Record on newsprint.*

   ✔ Based on the list we just created, how many of you now consider yourselves spiritual?

2. Invite each participant to select one word or phrase from the "Spirituality" list which he feels very comfortable or uncomfortable with and to explain in detail why he selected that item, then allow the group to share reactions after each monologue.

   ☞ *List the common reasons for participants' comfort or discomfort.*

3. Distribute sheets of newsprint, pencils, markers, and crayons and have participants draw their own "spiritual coat of arms"—a symbolic representation of the important aspects of his spirituality.

   ☞ *Forewarn them that they will be asked to share their drawing.*

©1995 Whole Person Press 210 W Michigan Duluth MN 55802   (800) 247-6789

4. Have each participant hang his drawing on the wall and explain its symbolic meaning to the entire group; allow others to ask questions.

5. Use the following questions to lead a discussion on how spirituality fits into our lives:

   ✔ What daily or semi-regular activities reflect your spirituality?

   ✔ Have you ever gone out of your way to do something because of your spiritual convictions? When?

   ✔ Have your spiritual convictions ever prevented you from doing something? When?

   ✔ How does your spirituality improve your quality of life?

   ✔ What steps can you take to increase your spirituality?

6. Close the activity by inviting each participant to begin action planning by identifying what he feels he should do to help increase his spirituality (e.g., "I should spend more time meditating").

10 SAME YET DIFFERENT

Designed specifically for members of the clergy, this introspective activity helps participants identify themselves not as "men of the cloth," but as individuals and men.

GOALS

To allow clergymen an opportunity to examine themselves as unique individuals and as men rather than simply by their profession.

To examine some of the specific problems and issues confronting clergymen.

TIME

1–1½ hours.

GROUP SIZE

6–24 participants.

MATERIALS

Newsprint; markers; tape; pens or pencils; crayons.

PROCESS

1. Distribute newsprint and writing instruments and ask participants to work by themselves and draw a picture of themselves as clergymen.

   ☞ *The drawings can be literal or symbolic.*

2. After five minutes, have participants hang the pictures around the room.

3. Have participants walk around the room for ten minutes, examining the pictures and noting similarities.

4. Brainstorm a list of the similarities they discovered, record it on newsprint, and lead a discussion based on the list.

5. Allow each participant a few minutes to stand next to his picture and describe it to the rest. Others can ask questions.

6. Distribute more paper and have participants draw a member of any other occupational group (from an actor to a zoologist), and hang their work on the walls when finished.

---

7. Allow participants five minutes to walk around the room noting similarities and differences between the two sets of drawings.

8. Form groups of six to share what they saw as similarities and differences and discuss them using the following questions:

    ✔ How did most of us portray members of other groups? Did you notice any clichés in the depictions?

    ✔ How did we portray ourselves?

    ✔ Does it ever bother you to be defined by the preconceptions and expectations of being a clergyman?

    ✔ What kind of problems does that cause?

    ✔ What can we do to overcome those conflicts?

9. Reconvene the entire group, and have the small groups report on the insights they discovered in their discussion, then close with a chalktalk based on the following statements:

    • Nobody likes to be defined by stereotypes about their profession, but as we all know, most people have preconceptions about members of clergy.

    • They expect you to be involved in limited types of activities, to behave in certain ways, and are sometimes even surprised to see you dressed in "street" clothes.

    • But, as we discovered today, we are all unique individuals, yet not all that different from any other man.

    • It is important for us to see ourselves as complete men, even if those around us don't.

VARIATION

■ This design can be adapted for any homogeneous group whose members are often defined by just one aspect of themselves—occupation, race, sexual identity—rather than their individual identities.

11 SINGLE MAN

Created especially for unmarried men, this exercise allows participants to examine what it means to them to be single and to develop strategies for the unique pressures of being single.

GOALS

To clarify our self-images as single men.

To understand the pressures of being single and how to cope with them.

To identify areas for personal growth and development as single men.

TIME

1½ hours.

GROUP SIZE

6–24 participants.

MATERIALS

Newsprint; markers; tape; writing paper; pens or pencils.

PROCESS

1. Initiate the exercise with a brainstorming session to create a list of images participants associate with being a single man.

   ☞ *Start them off with typical responses such as "free." Record the list on newsprint.*

2. Distribute paper and pens and ask participants to spend a few minutes listing the images that fit them or their life-style and assessing how these items fit with each other.

   ☞ *One visual way would be to do a "pie of my life" diagram.*

3. Form trios and have participants share and discuss their descriptions for about twenty minutes.

   ☞ *To help initiate discussion, ask how their descriptions may have changed in the past few years.*

4. Reconvene the entire group and conduct a brainstorming session to create a list of the pressures faced by single men.

5. Have trios combine to form groups of six, assign each group a specific pressure, and instruct them to identify strategies for coping with the pressure.

6. After fifteen minutes, reconvene the entire group and have each small group report the strategies they developed.

7. Ask participants to close their eyes and spend a few quiet moments imagining their ideal images of themselves as single men.

8. Reform the original trios and have participants share their images and create ways of achieving them.

9. After fifteen minutes, reconvene the entire group and allow each participant an opportunity to share what he has learned.

10. Close the exercise by having each participant complete the following sentence:

   • I'm glad I'm a single man because. . . .

12 FACING RETIREMENT

Participants examine their perceptions of retirement and assess their preparation for leaving the work force.

GOALS

To assess the assumptions we make about retirement.

To help make the transition from working life to retirement.

To examine impact retirement has on significant others.

TIME

1–1½ hours.

GROUP SIZE

10–30 participants.

MATERIALS

Newsprint; markers; tape; writing paper; pens or pencils; **Facing Retirement** worksheet.

PROCESS

1. Introduce the exercise and its goals with a chalktalk about retirement and the importance of planning for that transition.

    ☞ *Your introduction will vary according to the audience. This exercise is most effective if the majority of participants are in their fifties or sixties or if at least some individuals are approaching retirement age.*

2. Have each participant introduce himself and explain how close he is to retirement.

    ☞ *If some of the participants are already retired have them state how long they have been retired.*

3. Distribute the worksheet and allow ten minutes for participants to complete it.

4. Form groups of five or six to discuss their replies to the questions from Part 1 of the worksheet, which deals with how prepared they are for the transition to retirement.

5. After fifteen minutes, tell the groups to end their discussion and move on to the questions in Part 2, which focuses on how the participants' retirement may affect their wives or significant others.

6. After fifteen minutes, tell the groups to end their discussion and move on to the question for Part 3, which concerns the assumptions participants have made about how they plan to finance their retirement.

7. Reconvene the entire group and have a member of each small group report common assumptions their group made on the questionnaire.

   ☞ *Record these on newsprint.*

8. Close by providing statistical information that illustrates if participants' replies indicate they need to take more steps in preparation for retirement.

   ☞ *Gather up-do-date information from your local chapter of the AARP. You should also prepare a list with address and phone numbers of organizations in your area that can help your participants prepare themselves for retirement and make enough copies to distribute as they leave.*

FACING RETIREMENT

Part 1

1. If you would retire tomorrow name five activities (vacation, projects, new job, hobby, etc.) you plan to do in the first six months.

2. Do you have a hobby that takes more than five hours a week at present? Please describe.

3. How many jobs have you had in the last five years? These could be different jobs with the same company.

4. How many different companies have you worked for in the last twenty years?

5. How many times have you moved in the last ten years?

6. Do you plan on moving once you retire?

©1995 Whole Person Press 210 W Michigan Duluth MN 55802   (800) 247-6789

FACING RETIREMENT, continued

Part 2

1. How does your partner feel about you retiring? Have the two of you discussed it and how your roles will be different? Do you expect your partner to retire at the same time?

2. What assumptions have you made about retirement in general or about what your partner wants?

Part 3

1. What financial preparations have you made for your retirement?

13 GIVE YOURSELF STROKES

This closing exercise makes a positive and often powerful way to end a workshop or complete a series of evening sessions.

GOALS

To recognize self worth.

To receive honest compliments from others.

To gain experience in accepting compliments.

TIME

30 minutes to 1 hour, depending on the size of the group.

GROUP SIZE

Unlimited.

MATERIALS

Writing paper; pens or pencils.

PROCESS

1. Distribute paper and pens and instruct participants to list their strengths as well as those qualities they like about themselves.

    ☞ *Forewarn them that all will share their strengths verbally with the entire group.*

2. Have participants form a circle and give the following directions:

    ➤ Each of you will now read his list to the group.

    ➤ When you finish, say, "Does anyone have anything to add?"

    ➤ Other participants who think of a strength that the speaker did not list should mention it at this time.

    ➤ The speaker receiving a compliment should say "thank you" after each statement.

    ☞ *When the compliments stop move on to the next person. Continue until the entire group has shared their lists (including the trainer's). Do not tolerate any negative remarks.*

Conclude by reminding each participant that each of us has strengths and that it is important to recognize our own strengths as well as those of our friends and coworkers.

Adapted from Assertive Communications Skills Workshop, C&P Telephone, Baltimore.

©1995 Whole Person Press 210 W Michigan Duluth MN 55802   (800) 247-6789

SELF-DISCOVERY READING LIST

Baker, Mark. *What Men Really Think*. New York: Simon and Schuster, 1992.

Bednarik, Karl. *The Male in Crisis*. Greenwood, Conn.: Greenwood Press, 1981.

Bly, Robert. *Iron John: A Book About Men*. New York: Addison-Wesley, 1990.

Bolen, Jean Shineda, M.D. *Gods in Everyman: A New Psychology of Men's Lives and Loves*. San Francisco: Harper & Row, 1989.

Chew, Peter. *The Inner World of the Middle-Aged Man*. New York: MacMillan, 1976.

Fulgham, Robert. *All I Really Need To Know I Learned In Kindergarten*. New York: Ivy Book, 1988.

Gaglin, Willard, M.D. *The Male Ego*. New York: Viking, 1992.

Hudson, Liam, and Bernadine Jacot. *The Way Men Think: Intellect, Intimacy and the Erotic Imagination*. New Haven, Conn.: Yale University Press, 1991.

Keen, Sam. *Fire In The Belly: On Being A Man*. New York: Bantam Books, 1991.

Lee, John. *The Flying Boy: Healing the Wounded Man*. Deerfield Beach, Fla.: Health Communications, 1987.

Levinson, Daniel. *The Seasons of a Man's Life*. New York: Ballantine Books, 1978.

Meade, Michael. *Men and the Water of Life: Initiation and the Tempering of Men*. San Francisco: Harper of San Francisco, 1993.

Moore, Thomas. *Care of the Soul: A Guide for Cultivating Depth and Sacredness in Everyday Life*. New York: HarperCollins, 1992.

Morgentaler, Abraham. *Male Body: A Physician's Guide to What Every Man Should Know*. New York: Simon and Schuster, 1993.

Peck, M. Scott. *A World Waiting to Be Born*. New York: Bantam Books, 1993.

Porter, Lawrence, and Bernard Mohr. *Reading Book for Human Relations Training*. Arlington, Va.: NTL Institute, 1984.

Reid, Clyde. *Celebrate the Temporary*. New York: Harper & Row, 1974.

von Franz, Marie-Louise. *Puer Aeternus*. Boston: Sigo Press, 1981.

Consciousness
Raising

CONSCIOUSNESS RAISING

Consciousness raising groups, once primarily associated with the women's movement, emerged in the 1960s. They traditionally met once a week, with each meeting structured around a specific topic area and designed to increase the participants' awareness of feelings, behaviors, and experiences surrounding gender roles. The activities in a consciousness raising exercise are geared to generate discussions during which participants share personal experiences with other men in order to gain a better understanding of themselves and to find more positive directions for their lives.

Some of the benefits that male consciousness raising groups offer participants include:

- An opportunity for men to learn how to establish positive, healthy relationships with other men.
- An opportunity to make new friends: participants experiencing isolation and loneliness often find that those feelings dissipate; many experience a form of friendship or "buddyship" they have not known since college or even high school.
- An opportunity to experience a kind of impact and energy unique to an all-male group.
- An opportunity for men to get in touch with their anger and rage for the first time.
- An opportunity to validate their feelings: many participants sense that they are not crazy after all, that others have had thoughts and experiences similar to their own.
- An opportunity to explore alternative outlets and discover new, positive role models.

This section includes several designs to choose from to create a single session or a series. The outline below is just one example of how a trainer can plan five nonthreatening weekly sessions for small groups:

Week #1: Exercise 14, Boxed In: Male Stereotypes

Week #2: Exercise 16, Men's Lives

Week #3: Exercise 17, What Do I Do With My Life?

Week #4: Exercise 20, Get In Touch With Anger

Week #5: Exercise 22, Dreams

If the group chooses to continue beyond these five sessions, it can decide on its focus and possibly incorporate exercises from the other sections of this book.

A number of designs lend themselves to larger groups. Exercise 15, "Which One Is Me?" works best in a group of twenty or more. Exercise 16, "Men's Lives," can be used in either a small or large group, but Exercise 18, "Mr. America Contest," needs at least twenty participants to be effective.

The "anger" exercises (19, 20, and 21) require special mention. Anger is an extremely volatile subject for most men to discuss, a very sensitive area that most men have never allowed themselves to even become aware of, let alone explore introspectively. Because of this, the exercises included are designed to increase awareness. Only Exercise 19, "Anger: Warm-Ups," is experiential and then only in a limited way. If the facilitator wants to go further, and feels the group is prepared for more in-depth work, George Bach's *Fair Fighting* offers a number of excellent resources.

For some men, the very notion of joining a consciousness raising group is threatening. In those cases, starting at a less threatening point, such as discussions of books, might be appropriate. Many books are suitable, including *The New Male* by Herb Goldberg and *The Women's Room* by Marilyn French. The former is rather straightforward; the latter is a novel whose relevance could easily elude some men. In either case, the facilitator should work to steer men away from philosophizing about the books and toward identifying connections between themes in the books and their own experiences. (For detailed publication data on the books mentioned, see the Consciousness Raising Reading List on pages 86 and 87).

14 BOXED IN: MALE STEREOTYPES

By "acting out" stereotypes they identify with as well as those imposed on them, participants examine how these preconceptions color their behavior and attitudes.

GOALS

To examine and reflect on the stereotypes we identify with as well as those imposed on us.

To discuss the relationship of behavior to stereotypes.

TIME

1 1/2–2 hours.

GROUP SIZE

8–12 participants.

MATERIALS

Newsprint; markers; tape or safety pins; **Male Stereotype Label** cards.

PROCESS

☞ *Prior to the exercises, photocopy and cut out four sets of the* **Male** *Stereotype Labels* *on page 48-51. You should also write a list of those stereotypes on newsprint.*

1. Introduce the exercise and its goals with a chalktalk based on the following statements:

   • When we think of stereotypes, we usually think of others: other races, other genders, other age groups. Many of these stereotypes have negative associations.

   • We all have stereotypes we identify with; these, of course, generally have positive associations.

   • Today we are going to examine the stereotypes we associate with, those we impose on others, and the effects they have on our behavior.

2. Place one set of the **Male Stereotype Label** cards on a table and instruct participants to choose a label they identify with and secure it to their shirt.

☞ *Limiting the number of labels to one for each person in the group will force some uncomfortable choices.*

3. Have participants each take a turn explaining why they chose the label they assigned themselves.

   ☞ *If you think participants are comfortable with the idea, have them "act out" their stereotypes rather than simply explain them. This will also better prepare them for Step 5.*

4. Form groups of four and five and give each group a set of labels. Ask participants to choose a stereotype for each of their fellow group members and secure the labels on their colleagues. Each person will then wear three new labels.

5. Reconvene the large group and allow participants time to "act out" the stereotypes imposed on them by those in their group.

   ☞ *Participants usually portray one stereotype at a time, but you can add humor and insight by having them attempt to act out all three at once.*

6. When everyone has had a turn to perform, create a discussion using the following questions:

   ✔ What differences did you notice between the stereotypes you chose for yourself and those your group members labelled you with?

   ✔ What tensions were present when you had to act out more than one stereotype at a time?

   ✔ What caused you to select the labels you gave your fellow participants?

   ✔ Do the stereotypes you impose on others cause you to act in certain ways when you're around people you consider members of those groups? How? Why?

   ✔ Do the stereotypes you identify with affect your behavior in any way? How? Why?

   ✔ Did you learn anything new about yourself during the exercise?

VARIATION

■ Before closing, depending upon the emotional level of the group, it may be helpful to have participants "unhook" from the labels by destroying the cards.

©1995 Whole Person Press 210 W Michigan Duluth MN 55802   (800) 247-6789

MALE STEREOTYPE LABELS

CIVIC LEADER

GOOD PROVIDER

INTELLECTUAL

ARTIST

MALE STEREOTYPE LABELS

EXECUTIVE

BOSS

GOD'S GIFT TO WOMEN

JOCK

MALE STEREOTYPE LABELS

MOVER & SHAKER

FAMILY MAN

LABORER

GENTLE-MAN

MALE STEREOTYPE LABELS

MACHO MAN

LONER

SOLID CITIZEN

ALL AMERICAN

15 WHICH ONE IS ME?

Using four videos running simultaneously, participants are "bombarded" with imagery to help them identify themselves among generalizations of their gender. This exercises works effectively as a start to weekend programs, but is relatively costly to present because of the video rental fees.

GOALS

To dramatize the pressures on men.

To identify images or ideas we associate with ourselves.

To identify images or ideas that threaten us.

TIME

1½–2hours.

GROUP SIZE

6–24 participants (but be sure you have enough facilitators present to lead individual small groups of 6).

MATERIALS

Four sets of TVs and VCRs; the following four videocassettes: **1. Men's Lives** (Newday Films, 22D Hollywood Ave., Hohokus, NJ 07423; 201-652-6590; $50 rental); **2. Grab Hold of Today** (Ramic Productions, P.O. Box 9518, Newport Beach, CA 92660; 714-640-9115; $150 rental); **3. Keep Reaching: The Power Creative Media** (Creative Media, 11358 Aurora Avenue, Des Moines, Iowa 50322; 515-278-8213; $125 rental); **4. Vir Amat** (Multi-Focus, 1525 Franklin Street, San Francisco, CA 94109; 800-821-8514; $40 rental).

☞ *Caution: Vir Amat includes a graphic depiction of a male homosexual relationship and may be reacted to strongly by some heterosexual members of the group. Also, it is particularly important to allow participants enough time to debrief after seeing the films. Make sure you watch the films prior to the exercise.*

PROCESS

1. Introduce the exercise and its goals and explain that some images in the films may be unpleasant or even offensive to some, but that they are all an important part of the exercise.

2. Begin showing the films following the sequence below:

☞ *Showing all four films takes about one hour.*

   a. Begin with **Men's Lives.**

   b. After ten minutes, start **Grab Hold of Today.**

   c. After another ten minutes, start **Keep Reaching.**

   d. After about twelve minutes, start **Vir Amat.**

   ☞ *To simplify the exercise, you may want to omit either* **Grab Hold of Today** *or* **Keep Reaching.**

3. At the conclusion of the films, create small groups of six, assign a facilitator to each group, and have them spend thirty minutes discussing the impact of the films using the following questions:

   ✔ What was your general reaction to watching all four films at once?

   ✔ Which character or film did you most identify with the most? Why?

   ✔ Which character or film was the most threatening? Why?

4. Reconvene the entire group and, with a showing of hands, identify which characters or films the participants associated themselves with or were threatened by.

   ☞ *Record their reactions on newsprint.*

5. Use the list generated in *Step 4* to generate a closing discussion.

VARIATION

■ You might want to use material from Herb Goldberg's *The Hazards of Being Male* to help you create a closing chalktalk in place of *Step 5.*

16 MEN'S LIVES

Using a movie as food for thought to generate ideas, participants discuss society's definition of masculinity and redefine what masculinity means to them.

GOALS

To be more aware of the ways in which society's definition of masculinity has affected us.

To become aware of how our plans in life have been influenced by society's expectations of men.

To create a more positive and realistic definition for ourselves.

TIME

2 hours.

GROUP SIZE

Unlimited.

MATERIALS

Newsprint; markers; paper; pens or pencils; TV and VCR; videocassette of **Men's Lives** (Newday Films, 22D Hollywood Ave., Hohokus, NJ 07423; 201-652-6590; $50 rental).

PROCESS

☞ *Prior to the exercise you should watch the video, which explores the state of men in society today, to become familiar with it and to make notes for your introduction and discussion. It is about forty-five minutes long.*

1. Introduce the video.

2. Show the video.

3. Form small groups and discuss the film using the following questions:

    ☞ *List these questions on newsprint prior to the exercise.*

    ✔ How do you define "masculinity"?

    ✔ How does your definition differ from that of society's?

✔ Have you felt pressure to conform to society's male stereotypes?

✔ In what ways is society's definition of masculinity destructive?

✔ How do you feel about men who do not subscribe to masculine roles?

✔ How do you think women feel about such men?

✔ Have you ever had dreams or goals that you did not want to tell anyone because they did not fit the male image?

✔ How do you think competitiveness affects friendships between men?

✔ Realistically speaking, what "role options" do men have in this society?

4. After about thirty to forty-five minutes, distribute a sheet of paper to each group and instruct participants to consider the discussion they just had and write down a group definition of masculinity.

☞ *Clarify that the definition should reflect their insights and not the impositions of society.*

5. Reconvene the entire group and have someone from each small group read his group's definition.

☞ *List key points on newsprint.*

6. Using the points identified in *Step 5*, summarize the entire group's definition of masculinity and encourage participants to redefine themselves according to that new definition.

VARIATION

■ As an alternative to initiating discussion in *Step 3*, make photocopies of the discussion questions and have each participant write his answers before their discourse begins.

17 WHAT DO I DO WITH MY LIFE?

Using worksheets and group discussion, participants explore the balance between how they spend their time and how they would like to spend their time.

GOALS

To assess how we currently use our time.

To carefully consider how we want to use our time in the future.

To develop ways to make more time for ourselves.

TIME

1–1½ hours.

GROUP SIZE

6–24 participants.

MATERIALS

Newsprint; markers; tape; paper; pens or pencils; **Time and Activity** worksheets; **Circle of Time** worksheets.

PROCESS

1. Introduce the exercise and its goals with a chalktalk based on the following statements and rhetorical questions:

   - How many of you have enough time to finish all your daily tasks? How many of you have enough time left over to do everything you want to do?

   - Time is a priceless commodity, and we would all become rich if we could figure out a way to sell it.

   - No matter how well we manage to get things done, we could all use additional time to do more of what we want to do.

   - Today we are going to examine how we spend our time and develop ways to make more of it for ourselves.

2. Distribute the **"Ideal" Circle of Time** worksheet and ask participants to spend about five minutes plotting how they would ideally spend their time.

3. After everyone has completed their "ideal" time plotting, distribute the **Time and Activity** worksheets and give the following instructions:

   ➤ On the two **Time and Activity** worksheets, chart your activities for a typical weekday and for a typical weekend day.

   ➤ Use a check mark to indicate whether you were alone or with others during each time period.

   ➤ In the last row, total the hours that you spend alone and with family, coworkers, and friends.

   ➤ Answer the questions at the bottom of each worksheet.

4. When all are finished completing the worksheet, distribute the **"Actual" Circle of Time** worksheets and have participants take five minutes to fill it out.

5. Form small groups and have participants take turns presenting their worksheets to one another and discussing their replies using the following questions:

   ✔ Is there a good balance in the way you spend your time?

   ✔ Are you spending your time the way you want to?

   ✔ When was the last time you spent a weekend away from home and alone with your partner?

   ✔ When was the last time you spent a day with other men?

   ✔ When was the last time you spent a day by yourself?

   ✔ What have you done to give yourself more time to do what is important to you?

6. After about twenty minutes, stop the small group discussion and ask participants to pause to consider what they would like to have more time to do—some changes they would like to make—and to record these ideas on the back of their **"Ideal" Circle of Time** worksheet.

7. When most participants have finished their lists, reconvene the entire group and close with a brainstorming session to develop ideas that will help participants create more time for the things they want to do.

   ☞ *Record highlights on newsprint and allow participants to question one another and elaborate on specific details.*

©1995 Whole Person Press 210 W Michigan Duluth MN 55802   (800) 247-6789

TIME AND ACTIVITY

TIME	WEEKDAY ACTIVITY	ALONE	FAMILY	COWORKERS	FRIENDS
7:00					
8:00					
9:00					
10:00					
11:00					
NOON					
1:00					
2:00					
3:00					
4:00					
5:00					
6:00					
7:00					
8:00					
9:00					
10:00					
	TOTAL HOURS				

1. Did work dominate your entire day?

2. How much time did you spend alone?_____
   With family?_____ With friends?_____

3. Are you satisfied with this balance?

TIME AND ACTIVITY

TIME	SATURDAY OR SUNDAY ACTIVITY	ALONE	FAMILY	COWORKERS	FRIENDS
7:00					
8:00					
9:00					
10:00					
11:00					
NOON					
1:00					
2:00					
3:00					
4:00					
5:00					
6:00					
7:00					
8:00					
9:00					
10:00					
	TOTAL HOURS				

1. Weekends should be a time for rest and recreation. How much time did you spend resting?_____ Playing?_____

2. Are you satisfied with the way you spent this weekend?

3. What would you like to be different?

"IDEAL" CIRCLE OF TIME

Instructions: Imagine you could spend your day any way you choose. Think about the things that are really important to you. In the circle below estimate in a pie chart format how much time you would like to spend in each activity over the period of one week. Areas might include time spent with children, by yourself, with friends, with family, at work, etc. This will be your **Ideal Circle of Time**.

"ACTUAL" CIRCLE OF TIME

Instructions: Looking at the activities for the two days on the **Time and Activity** worksheet, try to estimate in the circle below how much time you actually spend in each activity over the period of one week. Use a pie chart format and include areas such as time spent with children, by yourself, with friends, with family, at work, etc. This will be your **Actual Circle of Time**.

18 MR. AMERICA CONTEST

In this challenging group activity, participants use a mock beauty contest to examine what they value about themselves and other men.

GOALS

To explore what attributes are important to us, both in ourselves and in others.

To explore what we really value.

To explore how we assess other men.

TIME

2 hours.

GROUP SIZE

20 or more participants (does not work well with small groups).

MATERIALS

Newsprint; markers; paper; pens or pencils; **Mr. America Adjudication** worksheets; **Contestant Biography** worksheets.

> ☞ *The trainer should be familiar with a group before introducing this activity because it can generate uncomfortable feelings among men who feel unsure of themselves.*

PROCESS

1. Introduce the exercise and its goals with a chalktalk based on the following statements:

   • We probably all have an image of what we consider the ideal woman: her interests, personality, intelligence, what she looks likes, etc.

   • But most of us probably haven't stopped to consider what the ideal man might be like.

   • Today we're going to have a little fun as we discover what we value about ourselves and other men.

2. Distribute paper and ask participants to take five minutes completing the following open-ended sentence listing as many positive attributes as possible:

- My ideal man is . . .

3. Select five men to compete for the "Mr. America" title and hand them each a **Contestant Biography** worksheet.

    ☞ *Use a random selection method or ask for volunteers.*

4. Select three others to judge the contest, give them each a **Mr. America Adjudication** worksheet.

5. Select one participant to act as the Master of Ceremonies, explain that the rest of the group will be the audience, and explain the contest:

    ➤ Before we begin, judges and contestants will meet separately to prepare.

6. Have each group meet from ten to fifteen minutes:

    a. Judges meet to create questions for each of the contestants.

        ☞ *Explain to the judges privately that the questions should be along the line of "If you could go anywhere, where would it be?" or "If you could do one thing, what would it be?"*

    b. Contestants fill out their worksheets and think of a way they can present one of their talents.

    c. Divide the audience into five groups. Assign each group a contestant to champion, and have them develop ways to cheer their man on.

        ☞ *Encourage the audience to support their favorite with yells, cheers, placards, or whatever other means they can think of.*

7. The contest:

    ➤ Round One: M.C. introduces each contestant by reading their worksheets.

    ➤ Round Two: Each contestant has two minutes to demonstrate a talent.

    ➤ Round Three: Judges ask each contestant a different question and contestants answer.

8. Allow the judges just three to five minutes to select the winner and privately tell the M.C. who they selected.

    ☞ *It is important not to let the judging get out of hand. The actual winner is not important. Discussing what was learned from the exercise, Steps 8–10, is the real heart of the session.*

9. Have the M.C. announce the winner.

10. Prepare for small group discussions by asking the following questions:

    ✔ Contestants, how did it feel to be displayed and judged by your fellow participants?

    ✔ Judges, what dilemmas did you face adjudicating your fellow participants.

11. Form small groups of eight to discuss what participants observed during the contest; write the following questions on newsprint to help generate dialogue:

    ☞ *If possible, make sure each group includes a contestant, a judge, or both.*

    ✔ Do you think you really got to know the contestants?

    ✔ What issues emerged during the contest?

    ✔ Considering your list of attributes for the "ideal man," did any of your items change? Would you like to add more? Remove some?

12. Close by reconvening the entire group and brainstorming a list of attributes for the ideal man.

    ☞ *This will generate more discussion as participants will inevitably disagree on some items. Allow the dialogue, but don't let it digress too much.*

MR. AMERICA ADJUDICATION FORM

Directions: Your job is to select "MR. AMERICA" from five contestants. Below appear the three major criteria which you will use to determine the winner. You will also receive a form from each contestant with additional information. It is up to your group to determine how to decide the winner. You can assign marks with point values from 1-20 in any one criterion, or use some other determinate.

	1	2	3	4	5
I. PHYSICAL					
Height					
Weight					
Clothes					
Hair Style					
General Appearance					
Beard					
Other					
II. TALENT/ACHIEVEMENTS					
Occupation					
Education					
Income Level					
Net Worth					
Involvement in					
Other					
III. PERSONAL AREAS					
Community					
Marital Status					
Number of Children					
Personality					
Religious Affiliation					
Other					

CONTESTANT BIOGRAPHY

Name _____

Age _____

Current Address _____

Place of Birth _____

Height _____ Weight _____

Chest Size _____ Waist Size _____ Biceps Size _____

Marital Status _____

Wife's Name _____ Number of Children _____

Occupation _____

Employer _____

Education Level _____ College Attended _____

Hobbies, talents _____

_____

_____

Community Activities _____

_____

_____

19 ANGER: WARM-UPS

This warm-up exercise contains three quick activities to lead into either of the two succeeding anger exercises. You may want to use only one of these warm-ups, depending upon the time available and the group itself.

GOALS

To start thinking about anger as an emotion.

To experience how we express or suppress our anger and rage.

TIME

15–30 minutes.

GROUP SIZE

Unlimited.

MATERIALS

None.

PROCESS

Activity 1: The Roar

1. Ask participants to spend five minutes thinking about something that makes them angry.

2. Ask participants to spend five minutes thinking about how they feel or react when they get angry.

3. Instruct participants to stand up and roar as load as they can.

    ☞ *Have them roar three or four times, perhaps at different volumes. Encourage them by saying "I can't hear you!" If participation is weak, move on to another anger warm-up activity; if it is strong, move on to Exercise 20 or 21.*

Activity 2: Getting Angry

1. Ask participants to pair up and spend five minutes each finishing the following sentence:

- I get angry when . . .

2. Have the pairs spend five minutes discussing what surprised them about what they said and what their partner said.

3. Repeat *Steps 1* and *2* using the following sentence:

- I stop being angry when . . .

  ☞ *If participation is weak, move on to another anger warm-up activity; if it is strong, move on to Exercise 20 or 21.*

Activity 3: It's Mine!

1. Instruct participants to find a partner and give each pair some object to work with.

   ☞ *Make the object something simple, like a notebook, towel, or glove. They just need something small they can both hold at the same time.*

2. Instruct the pairs to each hold one end of the object and take turns saying "It's mine!" as they attempt to take the object from one another.

3. After about two minutes, stop *Step 2* and have the partners spend a few minutes sharing with each other what they felt during their verbal and physical tug-of-war.

4. Reconvene the entire group and have participants use the following questions and spend ten minutes discussing how they handled their conflict:

   ✔ Did any of you stop and try to talk your way out of the conflict?

   ✔ Did any of you resort to physical force to take the object?

   ✔ Did any of you simply give the object to your partner?

   ✔ How many of you became angry?

   ✔ Is this the way you normally deal with conflicts?

   ☞ *This type of exercise is usually used in assertiveness training. Similar exercises can be found in George Bach's **The Aggression Workbook**.*

20 GET IN TOUCH WITH ANGER

A short lecture and worksheet activity serve to help participants understand how they react to anger and why they have difficulty expressing their
anger or express it inappropriately.

GOALS

To increase awareness of how men experience and express anger and rage
in different social and interpersonal situations.

To become aware of consequences of not expressing anger.

To consider changes in the way we express anger in different social
situations.

TIME

2 hours.

GROUP SIZE

6–24 participants.

MATERIALS

Newsprint; markers; tape; pens or pencils; **Anger Awareness** worksheets.

PROCESS

Activity 1: What Is Anger?

1. List the objectives on newsprint and ask participants what words or
   phrases come to mind when they think of anger or rage.

   ☞ *Record their replies on newsprint.*

2. Give the following chalktalk on anger:

   ☞ *This should take approximately fifteen minutes.*

   • Anger and rage are natural feelings. The way we deal with anger is
     conditioned through our social education. Besides the influence that
     parents and peers have had on our feelings toward the expression of
     anger, a large part of our reactions can be attributed to the media.

Much of this material was developed by Edward Dworkin of Columbia, Maryland.

©1995 Whole Person Press 210 W Michigan Duluth MN 55802   (800) 247-6789

Even though popular television shows such as **Donahue** celebrated the "Sensitive Male" during the 1980s, television, movies, and even some professional sports continue to project the macho image of real men as strong and violent but silent. This image offers a rather limited range of ways for us to deal with our anger and rage.

- By holding rage in instead of expressing it, we do great harm to ourselves. When we look statistically at the rate of homicides, suicides, accidents, and illnesses among men and women, we have some idea of how this inability to healthfully express our rage affects men. For example, women attempt suicide twice as often as men, but men "succeed" at their attempts twice as often, and the life expectancy of men is much shorter than that of women.

- A further complication for men is that we often have a hard time differentiating who we are angry with. Our anger may be with someone who is not present (e.g., parents, a boss, or coworker) but we express it toward whoever is with us at the moment. Or, our conflict may be an internal one—we are actually angry with ourselves—but again we project it on someone who doesn't deserve it. The result of this behavior is that the other person usually has no idea why we are carrying on the way we are and we get a reputation for being a "hothead" who "blows his cork" easily and should be avoided.

- Holding our anger in is the result of inappropriate social education. We fear the consequences of expressing feelings because our options for expressing those feelings are so limited, but overlook the consequences of keeping them locked in. We give ourselves a false identity—Mr. Nice Guy. We act out of fear: fear of being out of control (psychological and physiological consequences) or fear of being disliked by friends or held back in our jobs (social consequences).

- As a result, many of us use some form of passive-aggressive behavior such as:

  1. Sending mixed, ambiguous messages.
  2. Manipulating others through sickness or by finding other ways to get people to feel sorry for us.
  3. Forgetting.
  4. Miscommunicating.
  5. Procrastinating.
  6. Failing to retain what was learned during an interaction.

©1995 Whole Person Press 210 W Michigan Duluth MN 55802   (800) 247-6789

7. Playing "Rescuer"

8. Inducing guilt in others.

9. Intellectualizing, rationalizing, etc.

10. Refusing to give others the emotional attention they deserve.

11. Becoming cynical.

12. Playing the victim.

13. Exhibiting behaviors common to eating disorders.

- Instead of trying to clearly identify the roots of our anger and speaking assertively about it, some of us will engage in the following inappropriate behaviors while acting out anger toward others (more often than not, these will occur when the other person is weaker than us).

  I. Language Violence:

  a. Threatening.

  b. Going for the "emotional jugular."

  c. Storing up feelings and exploding.

  d. Changing the rules.

  e. Freezing up; refusing to talk.

  II. Body Violence:

  a. Hitting the other person.

  b. Scratching.

  c. Kicking.

  d. Using weapons (shooting, stabbing, etc.).

  e. Throwing a temper tantrum, including violence toward our own body.

  f. Punishing a child excessively.

- Our anger exercises will only touch the tip of the iceberg. As we become more and more aware of our feelings—more in touch with ourselves—we may allow ourselves to get in touch with our anger and its sources and begin to learn how to deal with it in more constructive ways.

3. Provide the following three definitions:

  ☞ *Write them on newsprint prior to the exercise so participants can refer to them in the next activity.*

  - **Experiencing Anger:** How you initially react physically when experiencing anger,—flushing, sweating, tensing the abdomen, jaw or fists, stammering.

- **Expressing Anger:** How you act out your anger—physically withdrawing, not talking, bitching to someone else, breaking material objects.

- **Repressing Anger:** How you avoid expressing anger—not rocking the boat, never showing anger directly, preoccupied with acting friendly and being liked by everyone.

Activity 2: Anger Awareness

1. Distribute the **Anger Awareness** worksheet and allow participants about thirty minutes to complete it.

    ☞ *Depending on the group, you may wish to select only certain areas of the worksheet for the activity.*

2. Form groups of three and have them spend about twenty minutes discussing the worksheet using the following questions:

    ☞ *Write the questions on an easel for the participants to use as a quick reference during the discussion.*

    ✔ Do you hide your anger from other people, do you express it verbally, or are you sometimes physically violent?

    ✔ What do you do with your anger and rage toward your wife or girlfriend? children? employer? friends? women? men? parents?

    ✔ How important is it for you to be a nice guy?

    ✔ How are your children disciplined?

    ✔ How do you rate on the following indirect ways of expressing anger:

    a. Psychological

    b. Physiological

    c. Social

3. Reconvene the entire group and ask for a showing of hands of those that hide their anger, those who express their anger verbally, and those who are sometimes physically violent.

    ☞ *Use Step 3 to segue into Step 4.*

4. Close with a chalktalk based on the following:

    - Obviously you now know much more about how you express anger.

- Of course, knowing how and why you express your anger doesn't mean you won't get angry again.

- Hopefully understanding more about our anger will help us avoid bottling it up inside or displaying it with verbal or physical violence.

  ☞ *For more about anger, see* Creative Aggression: The Art of Assertive Living *by George Bach and Herb Goldberg (publication data on P. 86).*

ANGER AWARENESS

Directions: This questionnaire is for your use alone. There will be a general discussion to share what you want to share.

1. **How do you experience anger inside you when you are angry with the following people?** (By experience we mean being in touch with and having an awareness of anger existing. Be as specific as possible.)
   a. spouse/partner
   b. specific children
   c. mother
   d. father
   e. brothers
   f. sisters
   g. friends
   h. supervisors (boss)
   i. coworkers
   j. men
   k. women
   l. YOURSELF

2. **How do you express anger toward:**
   a. spouse/partner
   b. specific children
   c. mother
   d. father
   e. brothers
   f. sisters
   g. friends
   h. supervisors (boss)
   i. coworkers
   j. men
   k. women
   l. YOURSELF

ANGER AWARENESS, continued

3. **How important is it for you to be very nice? (Don't rock the boat, go along with others, seem like a nice person.) How are you nice with the following people?**

   a. spouse/partner

   b. father/mother

   c. son/daughter

   d. friends

   e. supervisor (boss)

   f. employees

4. **How do you discipline your children?**

   a. verbal threats

   b. physical violence

   c. deprivation punishment

5. **Who tends to initiate/express anger in your family and how is it expressed by the following people?**

   a. YOU

   b. spouse/partner

   c. specific children

   d. mother

   e. father

   f. specific brothers and sisters

6. **How do you personally feel about experiencing (being in touch with) anger and expressing anger toward others in general?**

   a. experiencing

   b. expressing

©1995 Whole Person Press 210 W Michigan Duluth MN 55802   (800) 247-6789

ANGER AWARENESS, continued

7. **How do you rate yourself on each of these indirect passive ways of experiencing and expressing anger?** (Assign each a degree from 1-10—1 being absence and 10, overabundance.)

MODALITIES

A. Psychological

    1) sadness   _____

    2) scare, fear   _____

    3) depression   _____

    4) repetitious acts   _____

    5) fears that others will hurt me   _____

    6) confused thinking   _____

    7) unusual highs and lows   _____

B. Physiological (somatic)

    1) headaches   _____

    2) nausea   _____

    3) stomach aches   _____

    4) muscle aches & pains   _____

    5) ulcers   _____

    6) colitis   _____

    7) hypertension   _____

    8) asthma   _____

    9) heart disease

  10) rashes and other skin problems   _____

  11) other (identify)   _____

C. Body Language

    1) yawning   _____

    2) passing gas   _____

ANGER AWARENESS, continued

C. Body Language, continued

   3) stuttering _____

   4) itching _____

   5) blushing _____

   6) paling _____

   7) obesity (overeating) _____

   8) other (identify) _____

D. Language and other behavior

   1) sending confused, mixed, ambiguous messages _____

   2) forgetting _____

   3) procrastinating _____

   4) inducing guilt _____

   5) intellectualizing, rationalizing, being super-logical _____

   6) refusing to give praise _____

   7) being a cynic _____

   8) being a super NICE person _____

   9) withdrawing from others _____

  10) being overinvolved with others _____

  11) continually being hurt by others _____

  12) other (identify) _____

E. Sexual Domain

   1) not achieving an erection _____

   2) not maintaining an erection _____

   3) ejaculating prematurely _____

   4) failing to ejaculate _____

   5) demanding sex even though your partner resists _____

   6) lack of concern over your partner's satisfaction _____

21 WHERE DID I GET MY ANGER?

Using a worksheet bolstered by group discussion, participants examine how they learned to express anger, what shaped their responses to anger, and how their reactions to anger have changed over the years.

GOALS

To become more aware of how we learned to express our anger.

To examine how early childhood helped develop our responses to anger.

To analyze how expressing our anger has changed during our lifetime.

TIME

1–2 hours.

GROUP SIZE

6–24 participants.

MATERIALS

Newsprint; markers; pens or pencils; **Expressing Anger** worksheet.

PROCEDURE

1. List the objectives on newsprint and review them with participants.

2. Distribute the worksheet and allow approximately twenty minutes for participants to complete it.

3. Create groups of five and give them the following directions:

   ➤ Spend 20 minutes discussing your answers to the first 16 questions.

   ➤ Then take turns sharing your answers to questions 17–20.

   ➤ Finally, spend some time discussing the similarities and differences of your answers.

4. Reconvene the entire group and use the following questions to generate a closing discussion:

   ✔ Regarding question 17, how many of you thought you were more like your mom? Your dad? Are you happy about this observation?

   ✔ How many of you would like to change the way you express anger?

   ✔ How can you go about changing the way you express anger?

©1995 Whole Person Press 210 W Michigan Duluth MN 55802   (800) 247-6789

EXPRESSING ANGER

Experiencing Expressing Anger: Early Contributions

When you were very young (4-6):

1. Who usually initiated expressions of anger in your family?
       Mom?   Dad?

2. How did mom/dad express anger toward each other?
   Mom?

   Dad?

3. How did mom and dad respond to the anger initiator?

4. How did mom and dad feel about the angry confrontation?

5. How was anger between mom and dad resolved?

6. How did you personally feel when mom and dad expressed anger toward each other?

7. How did mom and dad express anger toward you?

8. How did you feel when anger was directed at you?

9. How did you respond to mom and dad when they expressed anger toward you?

10. How did you express anger toward mom and dad?

EXPRESSING ANGER, continued

11. How did you express anger toward other people in your family? In your peer group?

12. How did you feel when you expressed anger toward others?

13. How did you feel when you experienced anger but did not express it?

14. How did mom and dad respond to your anger?

15. How did persons identified in Question #11 respond to your anger?

16. What decision(s) did you make between the age of 4-6 about experiencing anger inside yourself? About expressing anger toward others?

17. Do you express anger more like your mom or your dad?

18. Have you noticed any changes in your anger and its expression as you grow older?

19. How do you feel about the way you handle your anger?

20. What would you still like to change in this regard?

22 DREAMS

Participants examine how the changes that have taken place in their lives have affected the hopes and dreams they once had and then redefine their goals according to how their lives have been altered.

GOALS

To identify and acknowledge significant changes in our lives.

To recognize the effects of those changes on our behavior, attitudes, and self image.

To explore new goals for the future.

TIME

1–2 hours.

GROUP SIZE

6–24 participants.

MATERIALS

Newsprint; markers; tape; pens or pencils; Robert Frost's "The Road Not Taken" (you can find this poem in most anthologies of American poetry or a collection of Frost's work); **Life Changes Inventory** worksheet.

PROCESS

1. Introduce the exercise and its goals with a chalktalk based on the following statements:

   • Most of us recognize that some of the hopes and dreams we had will probably never be achieved; for example, once you reach thirty, you're probably sure you're not going to ever play ball in the majors.

   • Many of us have dreams a little less lofty than that, but even those can escape our grasp.

   • Often we don't reach some of our dreams because of the way our lives have changed.

   • Today we are going to explore those dreams and the changes that prevented their realization, talk about the dreams we have achieved, and set our sight on new goals that reflect how we have changed throughout our lives.

©1995 Whole Person Press 210 W Michigan Duluth MN 55802   (800) 247-6789

2. Distribute the worksheet and allow participants approximately 20 minutes to complete it.

   ☞ *Give participants a time frame to consider, i.e., one, five, or ten years. Depending upon the group, (a group of recently divorced men generate very different responses than men married five years or more), you may want to use a different amount of years. You may also want to focus the worksheet by adding or deleting the characteristics in the left column.*

3. Form groups of six or eight and allow about twenty minutes for participants to take turns sharing their responses and discuss the similarities and differences of the effect change has had on their lives.

4. Read Robert Frost's "The Road Not Taken" to the entire group.

5. Ask participants to consider the poem as they write down the effects that their life's changes have had on their dreams.

6. After five minutes, split the groups into smaller groups of three or four and have each participant identify new or existing dreams or goals he wants to focus his energy on during the upcoming year.

7. Remind the groups of the exercise's goals and then have them spend ten minutes helping each other brainstorm specific ways of realizing the dreams they each identified in *Step 6.*

8. Reconvene the entire group and create a closing discussion by brainstorming basic steps they can take to ensure that they meet the goals they have set for themselves.

LIFE CHANGES INVENTORY

Characteristics	Lost or given up	Gained
Physical		
Emotional		
Relationships		
Abilities		
Opportunities		
Skills		
Possessions		

23 THAT'S MY DAUGHTER!

Using a short guided-imagery script, participants compare their attitudes about young women in general to their feelings about their own daughters as they mature; they also begin to examine feelings about growing older.

GOALS

To compare our thoughts about attractive young women with our feelings about our daughters.

To examine our feelings of how others look at our daughters as compared to the way we look at other people's daughters.

To examine our feelings as our daughters become young women.

To examine our feelings about growing older.

TIME

1 hour.

GROUP SIZE

6–24 participants.

MATERIALS

Newsprint; markers; tape.

☞ *This activity could become a deep emotional experience for some participants! Do not use it unless the group is very comfortable together and you have a great deal of experience and a solid background in psychology. Focus participants who do not have daughters on their feelings about young women and growing older.*

PROCESS

1. Introduce the exercise's goals and provide the following instructions:

   ➤ Select someone to be partners with and stand next to each other.

   ➤ We will start this evening by taking a fantasy trip.

   ➤ As I read a little fantasy story, I want you to let your mind wander, to allow yourself to completely envision my words.

   ➤ Find a comfortable spot, relax, close your eyes, and prepare to listen.

   ☞ *Allow participants time to get comfortable.*

2. Read the following guided-imagery script slowly, pausing long enough for listeners to visualize the scene you are describing.

Our fantasy begins on a warm June morning. You are driving along a street that passes the local high school. You pass several groups of young women and really enjoy how good they look. You single out one young lady and continue to stare—she looks wonderful. She wears tight jeans and a provocative top; she has a terrific tan and her proportions are just right. You let your mind wander about her: her legs, hips, the long hair draping down her back. She looks around and you recognize her as . . . YOUR DAUGHTER!

➤ STOP! Turn to your partner and share what you're feeling this very moment.

3. Have pairs join two others to create groups of six and use the following questions to discuss the guided imagery activity for about thirty minutes.

☞ *Write the questions on newsprint prior to the exercise.*

✔ What is the scariest thing about the fantasy YOU just had?

✔ Did it ever occur to you that when you fantasize about a young woman you are having fantasies about someone else's daughter? Does that make a difference?

✔ Do you have fears about your daughter growing up?

✔ Is there any behavior toward her that you want to change?

✔ Discuss any fears you have of growing older.

4. Reconvene the entire group and generate a closing discussion by asking the small groups to report their common responses.

CONSCIOUSNESS RAISING READING LIST

Bach, George and Herb Goldberg. *Creative Aggression: The Art of Assertive Living*. New York: Avon Books, 1975.

Blaker, Karen. *Born to Please: Compliant Women/Controlling Men*. New York: St. Martin's Press, 1988.

Carney, Clarke, and McMahon. *Exploring Contemporary Male/Female Roles*. LaJolla, Calif.: University Associates, 1977.

Edwards, Marie and Eleanor Hoover. *The Challenge of Being Single*. Los Angeles: Jeremy P. Tarcher, Inc., 1974.

Farrell, Warren. *The Liberated Man*. New York: Random House, 1974.

_____. *Why Men Are the Way They Are: The Male-Female Dynamic*. New York: McGraw Hill, 1986.

_____. *The Myth of Male Power: Why Men Are the Disposable Sex*. New York: Simon & Schuster, 1994.

French, Marilyn. The Women's Room. New York: Summit Books, 1977.

Friel, John, Ph.D. *The Grown-Up Man*. Deerfield Beach, Fla.: Health Communications, 1991.

Goldberg, Herb. *The Hazards of Being Male*. San Antonio: Nash Publishing, 1976. (also available in Signet paperback).

_____. *The New Male: From Self-Destruction to Self-Care*. New York: New American Library, 1980.

_____. *The Inner Male: Overcoming Roadblocks to Intimacy*. New York: New American Library, 1987.

Gray, John, Ph.D. *Men Are From Mars, Women Are From Venus*. New York: HarperCollins, 1992.

Halper, Jan. *Quiet Desperation: The Truth About Successful Men*. New York: Warner Books, 1988.

Hopcke, Robert H. *Men's Dreams, Men's Healing*. Boston: Shambhala, 1990.

Moore, Robert and Douglas Gillette. *King, Warrior, Magician, Lover: Rediscovering the Archetypes of the Mature Masculine*. San Francisco: HarperCollins, 1991.

Osherson, Samuel, Ph.D. *Wrestling With Love: How Men Struggle with Intimacy with Women, Children, Parents, and Each Other.* New York: Fawcett Columbine, 1992.

Pearson, Carol S. *The Hero Within: Six Archetypes We Live By.* San Francisco: Harper & Row, 1986.

Schaef, Ann Wilson. *Escape From Intimacy.* New York: Harper and Row, 1989.

Stroll, Clarice. *Female and Male: Socialization, Social Role and Social Structure.* Dubuque, Iowa: William C. Brown Co., 1974.

Tannen, Deborah. *You Just Don't Understand: Men and Women in Conversation.* New York: William Morrow and Co., 1990.

TRAINER'S NOTES

©1995 Whole Person Press 210 W Michigan Duluth MN 55802   (800) 247-6789

Sexuality
and Intimacy

SEXUALITY AND INTIMACY

As men grow in self-awareness, they become more in touch with their own feelings as well as those of others. This often affects their attitudes toward sexual relations and intimacy. Men may discover that sex is only a small aspect of a complete relationship.

As a result of the shifting attitudes toward sexuality since the end of the "Sexual Revolution" men have discovered the importance of emotion in relationships. At the same time, women have been encouraged to explore their sexuality. These changes indicate that men and women are getting closer on the significance of sex in their lives and their relationships.

Yet we are still far apart, and many men continue to be trapped by attitudes shaped by stereotypes and myths of male sexuality such as the "macho man"—a tough, love-'em-and-leave-'em kind of guy who uses women and discards them or a troubled bad-boy that beautiful "nice girls" find themselves hopelessly attracted to—role models that encourage destructive relationships.

Men experience sexual pressure because they often do not consider their sexuality within the wholistic context of their lives and relationships. Additional pressure stems from the natural desire in us all to be found attractive by others and by the media's presentation of attractive people. Men restrict themselves by blindly accepting what films, TV, and magazines depict as the "ideal man" instead of relying on their own judgment.

Furthermore, the increased awareness of sexual harassment in our society has helped cloud our ideas about sexuality and intimacy even as we strive to broaden our attitudes toward women. Behaviors once thought acceptable—gestures such as touching a woman's arm during conversation or complementing her attire—are now considered improper and offensive. The sexual harassment issue has caused a dichotomy among men: many struggle to understand the impact of their behavior and how to change it while others become even more entrenched in the traditional macho image, ignoring or unconsciously ignorant of the impact of their behavior.

Men tend to "sexualize" their relationships with women, perceiving sex as the goal of a relationship rather than just one facet of it. While sex enriches loving relationships, too much emphasis can block us from fully appreciating our partner. If we sexualize our whole concept of pleasure and sensuality, we cut ourselves off from other rich experiences.

The fast-paced lives many of us lead also shape our attitudes about sex. We drive in the express lane to work, hurry from one task to the next, eat fast food, and love fast. Often too fast. True sensuality requires slowing down. It means appreciating ourselves and others and being willing to give and receive pleasure in a number of ways. Fully exploring the senses can add richness to our lives and those of our partners. Exploring sensuality can bring men to a greater awareness of themselves and how they relate to others. And a deeper awareness of sensuality helps put our sexuality into a wider perspective.

Unfortunately, men often equate relating sexually with intimacy, but they are not the same. Sex can be an intimate form of communication— but it can also be an aggressive way to control. It can be an act of true caring and feeling, of deeply appreciating and sharing with another. It can also be used to cause deep emotional pain. It is a source of intimacy, but not the only source.

The essence of intimate communication involves a willingness to be vulnerable, probably the biggest cultural taboo for men. As children, most men learned "if you have feelings don't show them, or if you must, don't show them to those who are close to you or depend on you." The irony is that, with this message absorbed, men frequently find it hardest to share themselves with those for whom it is most important. The rewards of intimacy, nonetheless, are worth the risk .

The riskiest part of intimacy for some men is sharing with other men. Intimacy between males remains taboo in our society, and many hetero-sexual males fear that displaying closeness to another man may label them as homosexual. Although homosexuals have gained some accep-tance in recent years, much of society continues to view homosexuality in a primarily negative light. This prejudice allows men to participate in only one end of the sexuality continuum—the purely heterosexual. One source of the discomfort many men feel toward their gay brothers is the challenge they present: homosexuals are acting on feelings that hetero-sexuals may also have. Many men are reluctant to allow themselves to have positive feelings toward other men because they feel they might have to act them out sexually—exactly what many also assume they have to do with women. And popular media helps fuel our fear of intimacy between men, portraying it as acceptable only "in extremes": on the edge of death, in war, at a championship sporting event, or some other

©1995 Whole Person Press 210 W Michigan Duluth MN 55802   (800) 247-6789

dramatic time. If depth can be found in these situations, why not also in our daily lives?

Despite society's continued support of male sexual stereotypes, groups of men discussing sexuality today are more likely to discuss the sex they are not having rather than to provide locker-room reports of the women they've "laid." They converse about their fears over losing an erection, the pressure to satisfy their partner's needs, their fears of getting AIDS and other STDs, and confusion over how some seemingly normal behaviors can be labeled as sexually harassing.

This section offers a variety of ways to help men with the sexuality and intimacy issues discussed above. Most can be used for both gay and straight men (in fact, if the group is mixed, it can probably enhance learning for both groups). It is crucial that leaders working with the designs feel comfortable about their own sexuality, and know their own values. They must also be able to encourage participants in that same openness. It is good practice, if two or more leaders are going to use these exercises, to plan together carefully, including working out strategies for dealing with possible participant reactions.

The two most general designs are Exercise 24, "Sexual Scale," and Exercise 25, "My Sexual Values." Both make appropriate introductory exercises for any sexuality workshop. Exercise 26, "Sexual Fantasies," requires more trust among group members and should follow an introductory exercise. The issue of men's relationships with each other is covered in Exercise 27, "Who Are My Male Friends?" and Exercise 28, "My Male Friend." The latter requires more group trust, as does Exercise 29, "Fear Of Falling/Failing."

Two designs deal specifically with sensuality, Exercise 30, "Sensuality I: Alone" and Exercise 31, "Sensuality II: With Another." Both can be used in a variety of ways and are particularly effective if you use the films and videos as suggested. These exercises require a private, comfortable room and plenty of time. Exercise 32, "What Women Want From Sex" can be used fruitfully with groups of both men and women as part of a one-day workshop on gender relationships.

Our two newest exercises focus on issues that our society is finally beginning to address. Exercise 33, "Different, Yet Same," brings heterosexual and homosexual men together to examine what little difference truly exists between the groups. Exercise 34, "Sexual Harassment," helps raise consciousness of what sexual harassment really is and how to change harassing behavior in ourselves and those around us.

©1995 Whole Person Press 210 W Michigan Duluth MN 55802   (800) 247-6789

24 SEXUAL SCALE

This introductory exercise gets groups started with a worksheet that helps participants gauge their attitudes toward sex and identify areas of sexuality they wish to explore in future exercises.

GOALS

To better understand where each of us stands in our sexual development.

To discover which areas of sexuality we want to explore.

To provide an opportunity for men to discuss sex.

TIME

1 hour.

GROUP SIZE

6–24 participants.

MATERIALS

Newsprint; markers; tape; pencils; **Sexual Attitude and Behavior Scale** worksheet.

PROCESS

1. Distribute the worksheet and allow about ten minutes to complete it.

2. After participants have finished, form trios and ask them to discuss their worksheet answers using the following questions:

   ☞ *Post the questions on an easel for quick reference by participants.*

   ✔ Did any of your replies surprise you? Why?

   ✔ Did any of your replies make you uncomfortable?

   ✔ On how many statements did you circle a ten? How many were ones?

   ✔ On how many did you indicate you want to change?

3. After thirty minutes, reconvene the entire group and give them a few minutes to ponder the following reflection question:

   ✔ How did you feel while sharing personal information about your sexual concerns with other men?

---

4. Close by brainstorming a list of the sexuality concerns they would like to explore in future sessions.

©1995 Whole Person Press 210 W Michigan Duluth MN 55802   (800) 247-6789

SEXUAL ATTITUDE AND BEHAVIOR SCALE

Directions: No one else will see this worksheet. Circle the number on the scale where you feel you are now and use an arrow to indicate the direction you would like to go on the continuum. A "10" means you strongly agree with the statement; a "1" means you strongly disagree.

I get most of my sexual needs taken care of.

| 1 | 2 | 3 | 4 | 5 | 6 | 7 | 8 | 9 | 10 |

I believe I have an attractive body.

| 1 | 2 | 3 | 4 | 5 | 6 | 7 | 8 | 9 | 10 |

Others find my body attractive.

| 1 | 2 | 3 | 4 | 5 | 6 | 7 | 8 | 9 | 10 |

I must be in love to really enjoy sex.

| 1 | 2 | 3 | 4 | 5 | 6 | 7 | 8 | 9 | 10 |

I find I want to give and get pleasure equally.

| 1 | 2 | 3 | 4 | 5 | 6 | 7 | 8 | 9 | 10 |

I usually always climax during sexual activity.

| 1 | 2 | 3 | 4 | 5 | 6 | 7 | 8 | 9 | 10 |

I never fake climaxing.

| 1 | 2 | 3 | 4 | 5 | 6 | 7 | 8 | 9 | 10 |

I engage in a variety of sexual behaviors and activities.

| 1 | 2 | 3 | 4 | 5 | 6 | 7 | 8 | 9 | 10 |

Finding sexual fulfillment involves telling my partner what I like.

| 1 | 2 | 3 | 4 | 5 | 6 | 7 | 8 | 9 | 10 |

I communicate my sexual likes and dislikes to my partner well verbally.

| 1 | 2 | 3 | 4 | 5 | 6 | 7 | 8 | 9 | 10 |

I possess a great deal of knowledge of what turns me on sexually.

| 1 | 2 | 3 | 4 | 5 | 6 | 7 | 8 | 9 | 10 |

I am very comfortable touching and looking at my body nude.

| 1 | 2 | 3 | 4 | 5 | 6 | 7 | 8 | 9 | 10 |

Masturbation is healthy and a way to care for myself.

| 1 | 2 | 3 | 4 | 5 | 6 | 7 | 8 | 9 | 10 |

25 MY SEXUAL VALUES

Participants get to know one another in this introductory activity by discussing their sexual values, histories, and fantasies.

GOALS

To examine sexual values.

To let men share with other men some of their sexual experiences, values, and fantasies.

TIME

1½–2 hours.

GROUP SIZE

6–24 participants.

MATERIALS

Newsprint; markers; tape; writing paper; pens or pencils; **Sexual Values** worksheets.

PROCESS

☞ *Caution participants about confidentiality: "Whatever is shared in this room stays in this room!"*

1. Distribute paper and pencils and ask participants to:

   ➤ Record the total number of people you have slept with.

   ➤ Record the number of people you have slept with in the last year.

     ☞ *Do not have them sign their sheets. Collect them and put numbers on newsprint in descending order. Allow group to comment on numbers.*

2. Use the following statements to create an introductory chalktalk:

   • It looks like some of us will have much more to talk about tonight than others; then again, these numbers represent quantity, not necessarily quality, and quality depends on what you value.

   • Throughout the rest of this exercise, we're going to examine our values and take some time to discuss our sexual experiences and even our fantasies.

3. Distribute the worksheet and allow participants about ten minutes to complete it.

4. Create groups of four and allow participants about an hour to address the worksheet questions one at a time, with each participant taking a turn to share his answers.

> ☞ *Encourage people to share only what they wish. It is more important to discuss questions about feelings than to divulge personal information. Small group discussions will be the most powerful part of this exercise and could easily exceed one hour if the group feels free to share. It is important not to put values on comments or have participants make value judgments about other people's comments.*

5. Reconvene the whole group and ask participants to share what they learned during the exercise.

> ☞ *Typically you will get comments like: "I thought I was the only one to feel that way" and "I never shared these feelings with other men before."*

©1995 Whole Person Press 210 W Michigan Duluth MN 55802   (800) 247-6789

SEXUAL VALUES

1. Have you ever slept with a friend's partner? If yes, what did you experience afterwards? What do you think of other men who do?

2. Have you ever slept with someone who you knew was another man's partner? What were your feelings as you were doing it? Afterwards? What do you think of other men who do?

3. Have you ever had sex with a prostitute? How did you feel about it? What do you think of other men who do this?

4. Have you ever had a "zipless fuck" (from Erica Jong's book, *Fear of Flying*—a short, purely physical sexual encounter never to be repeated with the same person)? If your answer is no, do you ever fantasize about such an encounter? If yes, how did you feel?

5. Did you have premarital sex? If so, at what age the first time? How did you feel about it? How would you react to your son or daughter having sex before marriage?

6. How often do you have sex? Is this enough? Too much? Who usually determines whether or not you will have sex—the partner you are with or you? Is it a shared decision?

SEXUAL VALUES, continued

7. Do you ever withhold sex as a weapon in a relationship?

8. How often do you masturbate? How do you feel about this?

9. If married or in a lifetime partnership, would you consider having sex with someone outside the relationship? Have you had such experiences? What do you think of men who do? Of men who don't?

10. What are you most attracted to in a partner? What really turns you on?

11. Do you enjoy your sex life right now? What would improve it?

12. How important is fidelity in a relationship?

13. Have you ever fantasized about a relationship with another man? (or if you are homosexual, with a woman?) Have you ever had such an experience? How do you feel about it? How do you feel about men who do?

©1995 Whole Person Press 210 W Michigan Duluth MN 55802   (800) 247-6789

26 SEXUAL FANTASIES

This exercise—in which participants share and examine their sexual fantasies—can be fun and informative, but make sure you use it in a group with a high level of trust.

GOALS

To discuss sexual fantasies in a relaxed, nonjudgmental atmosphere.

To examine the effect of those fantasies on our interpersonal behavior.

TIME

1–1 ½ hours.

GROUP SIZE

6–24 participants.

MATERIALS

Newsprint; markers; tape.

PROCESS

1. Introduce the exercise and its goals with a chalktalk based on the following statements:

   • This session should be fun: we're going to share our sexual fantasies.

   • Not all of us are going to agree with each others' fantasies; some may be a little wild for us, others may seem run-of-the-mill to the more adventurous types, and many simply won't be our cup of tea.

   • Take, for example, the cliché fantasy of seducing or being seduced by a woman dressed as a cheerleader. Some of us may share that fantasy, but those of us with daughters who are cheerleaders might find it appalling.

   • So it's important not to judge one another: it's not a contest to find out who has the wildest fantasies; the idea is to have fun and really think about the role that fantasy plays in our sexuality.

   • And always remember: only you are responsible for what you say.

2. Brainstorm a list of common sexual fantasies—not necessarily those of

the participants—and record them on the newsprint.

> ☞ *Start with the cheerleader fantasy to get the ball rolling. Brainstorming assists in desensitizing participants that may be reluctant to share.*

3. Form small groups of six and have each participant take a turn describing his most frequent sexual fantasy.

4. After each has described his fantasy (about twenty minutes), have the small groups discuss the following questions:

> ☞ *Post the questions on an easel for quick reference by participants.*

✔ Have any of your sexual fantasies become reality? Would you care to explain? Did the experience live up to your expectations?

✔ How have your sexual fantasies affected your actual sexual encounters? Have they blocked communication with your partner? Enhanced it?

5. After thirty minutes, reconvene the entire group and discuss the questions:

✔ How did you feel when you were sharing your sexual fantasies with your small group of colleagues?

✔ Do you think it's important to act out your sexual fantasies? Why? Can it be harmful? How?

6. One by one, ask participants to make a summary statement about the role sexual fantasies play in their lives.

7. End by asking each participant to reply to the following:

➤ Pretend for a moment that women everywhere find you sexually irresistible; basically, that all the women in the world are yours for the taking.

➤ Finish the following sentence with the wildest sexual fantasy you can imagine:

"When I leave here tonight, I'm going right out and . . ."

27 WHO ARE MY MALE FRIENDS?

By taking the time to consider close male friends and their characteristics, participants identify what they value about friendships with other men and develop ways to create new friendships as well as to improve those they already enjoy.

GOALS

To identify our close friends and what makes them special.

To identify similarities and differences among our friends and ourselves.

To identify potential new male friends.

To identify current friendships we would like to change or improve.

TIME

1 ½ hours.

GROUP SIZE

6–24 participants.

MATERIALS

Newsprint; markers; tape; pens or pencils; **My Best Friend** worksheets.

PROCESS

1. Introduce the exercise with the following instructions:

   ➤ Think for a moment about who you consider to be your best male friend—the man you really feel close to and risk sharing personal feelings with.

   ➤ Don't consider just men with whom you work.

   ➤ Take a few minutes to quietly think about this man and what it is about him that makes him your best friend.

2. Distribute the worksheet and allow participants about fifteen minutes to complete it.

3. Form groups of four and allow them about thirty minutes to share their responses and discuss the worksheet using the following questions:

   ✔ Were you surprised at who you listed as close friends?

✔ Did you expect your list to be longer? Shorter?

✔ Is your best male friend very much like you or very different than you?

✔ How is your best male friend similar to your wife or partner?

✔ What is it about this person that makes his friendship important to you?

4. At the end of the discussion, hand out blank paper, and invite participants to make a list of men they would either like to be closer to or with whom they would like to begin a friendship.

5. When they are finished, have group members share their new lists, explaining why they selected the men they wish to be new or better friends with.

6. Reconvene the entire group and ask each participant to report his number of close friends, calculate the groups average, and record it on newsprint.

7. Generate a closing discussion with the following questions:

✔ How many of you have more close friends than you thought? Fewer?

✔ Why is it important to have close male friends?

✔ How can we get closer to some of the friends?

✔ What steps can we take to initiate friendships?

☞ *Turn the last two questions into a brainstorming session by keeping track of responses and asking participants to elaborate on their suggestions.*

VARIATION

■ Provide two worksheets for each participant, but have them use one to identify their best female friend and generate a list of close female friends. They can then compare the information. You could also repeat or substitute the exercise with focus on close women friends instead of men.

■ Have participants fill out a worksheet for several friends, and then allow time for them to examine the similarities and differences among the men they are close to.

©1995 Whole Person Press 210 W Michigan Duluth MN 55802   (800) 247-6789

MY BEST FRIEND

Name of your best male friend _____

1. Age

2. Physical appearance (tall, short, fit, out of shape, etc.)

3. Personality (outgoing, quiet, friendly, etc.)

4. Education

5. Occupation

6. How did your friendship begin and how long have you been friends?

7. How often do you meet and what do you usually do?

8. How is this person like/unlike you?

9. Do you feel comfortable calling this person just to say hello?

MY BEST FRIEND, continued

10. Do you feel comfortable sharing personal feelings with this person?

11. What needs of yours are met through this friendship?

12. What, in particular, makes this person a special friend?

13. What would you like to change about the friendship?

14. List below all the men you consider close friends.

28 MY MALE FRIEND

This exercise uses a guided imagery activity to allow participants to examine the values and rewards found in friendships with other men as well as identify their levels of comfort with close male friends.

GOALS

To identify the values and rewards in our relationships with other men.

To identify comfort levels in our relationships with other men.

TIME

1–1½ hours.

GROUP SIZE

6–24 participants.

MATERIALS

None.

PROCESS

1. Begin the exercise by having participants brainstorm attributes they associate with the word "friend."

2. Form small groups and generate a thirty-minute discussion with the following questions:

   ✔ How does it feel to be introduced by a friend as "my pal" or "my buddy"?

   ✔ What do you get from your relationships with other men?

   ✔ Do you ever cultivate friendships with men to get specific rewards (business connections, event tickets, etc.)? How does that make you feel?

   ✔ Have you ever had a friend that spent time with you to get these same kinds of rewards? How did that make you feel?

3. Reconvene the entire group and ask participants to find a comfortable place in the room to sit or lie down.

   ☞ *Dim the lights if possible. Encourage them to breathe slowly and deeply.*

4. When everyone seems comfortable and relaxed, read the following guided imagery script:

   ☞ *The questions in the script are a guide. You may add to or delete any of them—remember, you are directing the fantasy.*

   Close your eyes and imagine your "best" male friend. Think for a moment about what you know about him. Can you imagine him as a youth-growing up? Can you remember your first meeting? Your first impressions? Picture the friend slowly approaching. What do you notice about him? How do you greet—with a handshake? a hug? a kiss? Do you walk together? stand? sit? How close do you get physically? Where are you? What are you talking about? Picture the two of you going to one of your houses or apartments. What happens? What do you do together? What are your feelings about being alone with your friend? Picture your friend leaving. How do you feel when this happens? What are your feelings when you do not see your friend for a long period. Take a few minutes and really think of what you do and how you feel when you spend time with him.

   ☞ *End the exploration after five minutes, but allow participants time to "recover." Some may feel tense, others relaxed, so they need a moment or two to get "back into" the group.*

5. Close with a discussion about their feelings during the guided imagery activity using the following questions:

   ✔ Where you surprised at anything you visualized?

   ✔ At what point did you feel most relaxed? Most uncomfortable?

   ✔ Did the activity make you think of ways you want to behave differently with your friend in the future? How? Why?

   ☞ *You may wish to record what was learned on an easel sheet.*

29 FEAR OF FALLING / FAILING

Participants explore times when they feel weak and discuss the benefits of expressing their feelings as opposed to keeping them bottled up.

GOALS

To identify some of our innermost feelings.

To share our feelings and assess their effect on ourselves and others.

To understand how we become blocked from sharing our feelings, especially those that might make us seem weak.

TIME

1–1½ hours.

GROUP SIZE

6–24 participants.

MATERIALS

Newsprint; markers; tape; writing paper; pens or pencils.

PROCESS

1. Prepare the group by having them take deep breaths and then make louder and louder sounds as they exhale each breath. Ask them how it felt to release with increased effort, and then tell them:

   • Today we will explore how we hold feelings in and how we can let them out just as easily as we let out our breath, and with as much exuberance as we put into making those sounds.

2. Use a brainstorming session to generate a definition of the "strong, silent type."

   ☞ Record on newsprint.

3. Distribute paper and pens and have participants spend five to ten minutes creating a list of when they have felt weak, sad, frustrated, or depressed—when they simply do not feel strong.

4. Form trios to spend thirty minutes sharing their reactions and discussing items they hold in common as well as those that are different.

5. Reconvene the entire group and discuss the following questions:

✔ What are the benefits of expressing your feelings?

✔ What are the costs of suppressing your feelings?

✔ What then is so good about being the "strong, silent type"?

✔ What steps can we take to become more expressive about our feelings?

6. Close by having each participant complete the following open-ended sentence:

• I am strong, but sometimes I . . .

And encourage the group to affirm each statement by adding:

• And that's OK!

30 SENSUALITY I: ALONE

Using a different approach to common activities along with a short, funny film, participants examine the role of sensuality in their lives and consider ways to increase the opportunities to give themselves pleasure.

GOALS

To experience slowing down the pace of our lives.

To appreciate the pleasure of everyday occurrences.

To give ourselves pleasure in, perhaps, new ways.

TIME

1 hour.

GROUP SIZE

Unlimited.

MATERIALS

Pencils or pens; tape; 4"x6" cards; oranges; TV and VCR; the film **The Orange** (Multi-Focus, 1525 Franklin Street, San Francisco, CA 94109; 800-821-8514; $25 rental).

PROCESS

1. Warm up the group by distributing the cards and asking participants to take two full minutes to write their names*once*, without lifting their pen from the card the entire time.

2. Have participants secure their cards to their shirts as name tags and then walk around in silence as slowly as they can for five minutes.

3. Reconvene the group and spend ten minutes discussing their "slowing down" with the following questions:

   ✔ What was it like to write that slowly?

   ✔ As you walked around, what did you notice about other people's name tags?

   ✔ Did you feel strange as you walked around? How?

   ✔ Did your colleagues appear as though they felt strange?

✔ Did you find slowing down pleasurable or uncomfortable?

☞ *Add other questions that seem appropriate.*

4. Pass out oranges and ask each person to spend a few minutes becoming more familiar with his orange (but not to eat it!).

5. Show **The Orange** (takes about two minutes).

6. Invite participants to explore their oranges again.

7. Have a brief discussion on the effects of the film on their "encounters" with their oranges and let them to begin eating their oranges.

☞ *Allow participants ample time to enjoy their oranges.*

8. Form groups of six to eight to describe the pleasure of eating the orange.

9. Close with a chalktalk based on the following statements:

- We all seemed to have a pretty good time just taking a few minutes to slow down and do things a little differently.

- Many of the activities we do every day can be calming, sensuous experiences if we allow ourselves enough time to enjoy them as such.

- For example, taking a bath or a shower, eating, drinking something we enjoy—all of these can be very sensuous activities if we focus on them instead of rushing through them.

- Try to find the time to make one activity each day a calm, sensuous moment.

31 SENSUALITY II: WITH ANOTHER

Using nonverbal communication, participants examine the importance of relating to and heightening their awareness of others.

GOALS

To heighten our awareness of ourselves and others.

To explore a variety of ways of relating to others.

TIME

1 hour.

GROUP SIZE

6–24 (works best with an even number of participants).

MATERIALS

None.

PROCESS

1. Begin by asking participants to mill about the room without speaking looking first at the floor, then at each others' feet, legs, hands, torsos, head, faces, and finally, eyes.

2. Reconvene the group and ask them to close their eyes and silently consider:

   ✔ How many men are in the group?

   ✔ How many are wearing tennis shoes?

   ✔ How many have brown hair, black hair, etc.?

   ✔ How many have blue eyes, brown eyes, etc.?

   ☞ *Add any other questions that help to focus on the group in their environment.*

3. Have participants open their eyes and check their answers.

4. Use the following chalktalk points to introduce the rest of the exercise:

   • How well did you score? More right than wrong? Wrong than right?

   • Most of us probably didn't do too well. In general, people don't pay very close attention to details when they look at one another.

- Knowing the little things about each other, however, is important to how effectively we communicate with one another.

- During the remainder of this activity, we are going to get to know each other better through some nonverbal activity.

5. Pair up participants and have them sit face to face and spend five minutes completing the following open-ended sentences:

    ☞ *Post the sentences on an easel for quick reference by participants.*

- "I am aware that you have . . ."

- "I am aware that you have . . . and I feel . . ."

- "I am aware that you have . . . and I wonder if . . ."

    ☞ *Let partner respond. This can be repeated two or three times.*

6. Reverse partner roles and repeat *Step 5*.

7. Create new pairs and have them sit back-to-back. Ask them to spend five minutes expressing a variety of actions and/or emotions nonverbally. Start with a greeting and end with a good-bye, expressing themselves only with their backs, shoulders, and heads—no hands!

8. Reconvene the entire group for a closing discussion using the following questions:

   ✔ Was it difficult to find ways to express yourself nonverbally?

   ✔ Was it easy to understand what your partner was trying to convey?

   ✔ How did it feel to communicate this way?

   ✔ What steps can we take to become more aware of others and improve how we relate to them?

VARIATION

- ■ Depending on time and the tenor of the group, you may want to add a body-sculpting activity that can provide some fascinating insights. Form pairs and have one partner stand still while the other partner "chips" or "cuts" away at him to produce a statue. Reverse roles and end with a discussion using questions such as: What was the most difficult part to sculpt? What did you *not* sculpt? etc.

- ■ If your group is extremely comfortable with one another, try this foot washing activity as the final step: Form pairs, ask participants to take turns washing each other's feet, finishing with a gentle foot massage (body oil optional). Call group together to reflect on the whole session.

To close in a fun, nonverbal way, have everyone lie down in a circle, stick all their feet in the middle, and rub them all over each other!

32 WHAT WOMEN WANT FROM SEX

By comparing lists of what they think women want (and don't want) during sex, participants examine how their preconceptions influence their sex lives.

GOALS

To share some male perceptions about women's attitudes toward sex.

To understand the basis of these perceptions.

To see how these perceptions influence our sexual relations.

TIME

1–1½ hours.

GROUP SIZE

6–8 participants.

MATERIALS

Newsprint; markers; tape; writing paper; pens or pencils.

PROCESS

1. Distribute paper and writing instruments and instruct participants to make individual lists of what they think women in general want from sex (in terms of attitudes, behaviors, and practices).

   ☞ *Ask them to be as specific as possible.*

2. After five minutes, instruct them to make a list of what women *don't* want concerning sex.

3. Ask participants to spend five minutes examining their lists and then identify:

   a. One woman they know for whom the majority of the items on their list are true; and

   b. The source of their information (parents, friends, books, movies, TV, "the street," etc.).

4. Form pairs to discuss their lists.

5. Reconvene the entire group and create a master list on newsprint from the participants' lists generated in *Steps 1* and *2*.

☞ *Ask participants to refrain from making comments at this point.*

6. Create groups of three or four to discuss the master list and how their preconceptions have affected their behavior during sex. Use the following discussion questions:

✔ Which items on the list do you know to be wrong?

✔ Which items on the list are accurate according to your experience?

✔ Are some of the items wrong in some cases but accurate in others?

✔ Do the items you listed influence your behavior during sexual encounters? How?

✔ Since we now realize that many of our preconceptions are misconceptions, what can we do to prevent those ideas from affecting our sexual behavior?

7. Reconvene the entire group and have the small groups share the ideas they developed for changing their preconceptions and behavior during sexual encounters in the future.

Adapted from Male Sexuality *by Bernie Zilbergeld.*

33 DIFFERENT YET SAME

Gay and straight participants join to examine their similarities and differences and discover they have more in common then they may have thought.

GOALS

To allow heterosexual and homosexual men to understand each other better.

To show that, no matter what differences exist, all men have a great deal in common.

TIME

1–1½ hours.

GROUP SIZE

6–24 participants.

MATERIALS

Newsprint; markers; tape; pens or pencils; crayons.

> ☞ *This exercise works best when the group is made up of an equal (or close to equal) number of homosexual and heterosexual participants, and when the gay members are "out" and willing to discuss their sexual orientation and issues surrounding it. Keep in mind that you may have some participants who are defensive about their sexuality, so be alert and ready to keep issues from becoming personal and to direct discussions in ways that will reduce tension and conflict.*

PROCESS

1. Distribute newsprint and writing instruments and ask participants to work alone and draw a picture of themselves.

   > ☞ *The drawings can be literal or symbolic.*

2. After five minutes, have participants hang the pictures around the room.

3. Ask participants to walk around the room for ten minutes, examining the pictures and noting similarities.

4. Brainstorm a list of the similarities they discovered, record it on newsprint, and lead a discussion based on the list.

5. Distribute writing paper and have each participant spend five minutes listing activities they participate in or are interested in becoming involved with (sports, hobbies, organizations they belong to, books or magazines they read, etc.).

   ☞ *While they are making their lists, hand each participant his drawing.*

6. Form small groups of six, with an equal number of heterosexual and homosexual members, and have each person spend a few minutes describing his picture and reading his list.

7. Allow the groups thirty minutes to discuss their similarities and differences using the following questions:

   ☞ *Post the questions on an easel for quick reference by participants.*

   ✔ How did most of us portray ourselves? Did you notice any clichés in the depictions?

   ✔ Are there any visual differences, between one group and the next, in the way we depicted ourselves?

   ✔ Were there any activities on our lists common to only one group?

   ✔ Were you surprised by how much both groups have in common?

   ✔ Gay participants, does it bother you to be defined by preconceptions?

   ✔ Straight participants, have you ever felt defined by preconceptions? How did that feel?

   ✔ What kind of problems do stereotyped views of members of particular groups cause?

   ✔ What can we do to overcome our preconceptions of one another?

8. Reconvene the entire group and have the small groups report on the insights they made in their discussion, then close with a chalktalk based on the following statements:

   • Nobody likes to be defined by stereotypes but as we all know, most people have preconceptions about gay men and straight men.

   • We expect each other to behave in a certain way or have certain interests.

   • But, as we discovered today, we are not all that different from one another; in fact, except for our sexual orientation, we are very much the same.

- Remember that it is important for us to see ourselves as complete men, even if those around us don't.

34 SEXUAL HARASSMENT

Using a film and discussion revolving around brainstorming sessions, participants help each other become more sensitive to sexual harassment.

GOALS

To share male perspectives on sexual harassment.

To identify our feelings about the issue.

To share experiences involving accusations of sexual harassment.

To identify ways of supporting each other in relation to women in the workplace.

TIME

2 hours.

GROUP SIZE

6–24 participants.

MATERIALS

Newsprint; markers; tape; writing paper; pens or pencils; TV and VCR; the film **Shades of Gray, Part II: What is Sexual Harassment?** (Pacific Resources Development Group, 4044 NE 58th, Seattle, WA 98105; (206) 782-7015; $400)

PROCESS

1. Introduce the exercise and its goals and initiate a brainstorming session by having men react to the term "sexual harassment."

    ☞ *Record on newsprint. If the list contains few examples, you may want to suggest some of the following:*

    • *pressure for dates*

    • *sexual jokes or remarks*

    • *obscene language with sexual overtones*

    • *patting, touching, pinching*

    • *sexual gestures*

    • *promises of rewards for sexual conduct*

2. Create groups of six and have them discuss following questions for twenty-minutes:

   ✔ Do you agree with all the items on the list?

   ✔ Have you ever been accused of sexual harassment? If so, what were your reactions?

   ✔ Has anyone you know ever been accused of sexual harassment? If so, what were your reactions?

   ✔ Do you know of a case where you think someone should have been accused of sexual harassment? If so, what were the circumstances?

3. Reconvene the entire group and show the video **Shades of Gray**.

4. After the film, have the group create a list of behaviors they consider sexually harassing and record it on newsprint.

5. Lead a problem-solving discussion on how to determine if "gray area" behaviors are offensive or fit into the category of "unwelcome conduct."

6. Have the group consider the notion of men harassing men by contributing to a list entitled "Male Behavior in the Workplace that Bothers Me" and discussing the items they put on the list.

7. By using the following questions, discuss how men can support each other in the workplace:

   ✔ How can we make each other aware of offensive behavior before the problem gets out of hand?

   ✔ How can we change the behavior of a male colleague who refuses to listen to our concerns?

   ✔ How can we begin a dialogue with women that gives us clear feedback on our behavior or that of our colleagues?

   ✔ How can we transform our workplace behavior so that women will feel like partners and not objects?

8. Close the exercise by asking each man to commit to one thing he will do differently in the workplace to reduce or prevent sexual harassment.

SEXUALITY READING LIST

Doyle, J. *The Male Experience, 2nd Edition.* New York: William Brown, 1989.

Hite, Shere. *Hite Report On Male Sexuality.* New York: Ballatine Book, 1982.

Kelly, Susan Curtin. *Why Men Commit.* Holbrook, Mass.: Bob Adams, Inc., 1991.

Kivel, Paul. *Men's Work.* New York: Ballantine Books, 1992.

Lewes, Kenneth. *The Psychoanalytic Theory of Male Homosexuality.* New York: Simon and Schuster, 1988.

Miller, Stuart. *Men and Friendship.* San Lendoro, Calif.: Gateway Books, 1983.

Monick, Eugene. *Phallos: Sacred Image of the Masculine.* Toronto: Inner City Books, 1987.

Pittman, Frank, M.D. *Man Enough.* New York: Berkley Publishing, 1993.

Rhodes, Richard. *Making Love.* New York: Simon and Schuster, 1992.

Ross, John Munder, Ph.D. *The Male Paradox.* New York: Simon and Schuster, 1992.

Wyly, James. *The Phallic Quest: Priapus and Masculine Influence.* Toronto: Inner City Books, 1989.

Zilbergeld, Bernie. *The New Male Sexuality.* New York: Bantam Book, 1992.

TRAINER'S NOTES

Parenting

PARENTING

This section helps men examine their feelings about being parents. Most participants join parenting groups because they wish to become better fathers. Since few people successfully alter their behavior until they understand its origin, these exercises are designed to provide participants with a greater understanding of how they parent. The exercises may open doors to exciting and frightening discoveries, but with their new-found knowledge, participants can try new techniques or change behaviors when they find them appropriate. The exercises examine how men parent, society's expectations of fathers, and some basic dilemmas fathers encounter through various stages of parenthood.

Since most men learn about fathering from their own fathers, the first two exercises allow participants to examine how their fathers raised them. Exercise 35, "In Touch With Our Fathers," concentrates exclusively on the relationship between participants and their fathers while Exercise 36, "My Father/I Father," helps participants remember what they have learned from their father and decide what aspects of that knowledge they wish to employ or discard as they raise their own children.

The next three exercises concern one of the most important aspects of fathering—participants' behavior as role models for their children. Exercise 37, "I, Role Model," explores the values participants pass on to their children and Exercise 38, "Super-Dad," helps them settle the conflicts between what is expected of them as fathers and their own desires. Exercise 39, "Roles We Cast Our Children In," helps participants become more aware of how their perceptions tend to cast their children into certain familial roles.

Exercise 40 provides trainers with an activity to help a very specific group: men who are about to become fathers. "Pregnant Fathers" encourages participants to explore their hopes, fears, and anxieties about their impending fatherhood and to prepare to adjust to a major change in life-style.

The final three exercises help divorced or separated fathers deal with the conflicts that arise as they move away from their children. After a separation or divorce, many men realize how much they miss their children and how little "quality time" they spent with them while married. Ironically, after a divorce, men often feel able to give their children more attention then they did when married. They often want to spend more time

©1995 Whole Person Press 210 W Michigan Duluth MN 55802   (800) 247-6789

with their children, yet find themselves frustrated about the issues of child support and custody (although more and more men now seek custody, women win the overwhelming majority of custody cases).

All parents want to see their children well taken care of, well fed, and living in a good home. Conflicts arise, however, when they feel their former spouses do not let them spend adequate time with their children or when the parent paying support does not think his or her money is being well spent. These problems are compounded by the issues that originally caused the separation. Separated parents must learn, therefore, to distinguish their anger with their spouse from how they relate to their children. Exercise 41, "What Do I Get For My Money?" and Exercise 42, "Fathering: Separated Children," helps separated fathers do just that, and Exercise 43, "Fathering: Stepchildren," helps participants handle similar conflicts when they find themselves parenting their partner's children from a previous relationship.

To create a one or two day workshop on parenting, begin with an introductory exercise and then present the first five parenting exercises in the sequence they are presented here. If time permits, find out the group's special needs, form subgroups, and use appropriate exercises for expectant or separated fathers.

This design is an adaptation of work by by Glen Gaumnitz and Michael Nord.

35 IN TOUCH WITH OUR FATHERS

In order to better understand how they parent their own children, participants use discussion and a guided imagery activity to recall how their
fathers raised them.

GOALS

To better understand how we remember childhood experiences with our
fathers.

To convert what we remember of our relationships with our dads to an
understanding of how we raise our children.

TIME

1 1/2–2 hours.

GROUP SIZE

6–24 participants.

MATERIALS

Newsprint; markers; paper; pens or pencils.

PROCESS

1. Introduce the exercise with a chalktalk based on the following
   statements:

   - One of the strongest influences on how we parent our own children
     is how we were raised by our parents.

   - So in order to better deal with our own children, it is important to
     examine our own childhood.

   - Since we are men, our parenting tends to be more influenced by how
     our fathers helped raise us.

   - This exercise will give us a chance to recall how our fathers raised
     us so we can better understand how we make choices about the way
     we raise our kids.

2. Form small groups, distribute writing material to one member of each
   group, and provide fifteen minutes to discuss and create definitions that
   answer the following questions:

✔ What does "father" mean to me?

✔ What makes a man a father?

3. Reconvene the large group and have small groups report their definitions; record the highlights on newsprint and create new definitions based on the information culled from each group.

4. Lead the participants through the following guided imagery script:

☞ *It is important to make sure participants are relaxed. Have them find a comfortable place in the room by themselves, either in a chair or sitting or lying on the floor, close their eyes, and relax. You may wish to lead them through some basic breathing exercises to help them relax. Allow a few moments between each question in the visualization. Add others that may be relevant to the group.*

Think about your childhood. . . . What is the first thing you remember about your father? . . . What did he smell like? . . . What do you remember doing with your father? . . . What happened when your father came home from work? . . . What was the best time you had with your father? . . . What was the worst? . . . When were you afraid of your father? . . . When were you the most proud? . . .

☞ *As you end the fantasy, have the participants open their eyes and rejoin the group as they feel ready. You may wish to have participants jot down what they remember.*

5. Distribute writing materials and have participants take ten minutes to write a letter to their father based on what they thought about during the guided imagery activity.

☞ *Tell them their letters can ask questions of their fathers, express gratitude, vent anger, or cover a variety of issues.*

6. Form small groups of six and allow them forty-five minutes to share and discuss their letters.

☞ *Since their letters may address highly-personal issues, let them know they can share just the parts of the letter they feel comfortable discussing with the group.*

7. Reconvene the entire group and brainstorm a list of what they learned about parenting from their fathers.

36 MY FATHER / I FATHER

By creating lists and completing a worksheet, participants compare their fathering skills with their fathers' and develop strategies for becoming more effective parents.

GOALS

To examine the similarities and differences between how we parent and how our fathers raised us.

To examine whether we want to change some aspects of our fathering.

TIME

1–1½ hours.

GROUP SIZE

6–24 participants.

MATERIALS

Paper; pens or pencils; **Fathering Characteristics** worksheet.

PROCESS

1. Distribute writing materials and begin by having participants use the questions below to generate a list of the positive and negative aspects they remember about their fathers while growing up:

   ✔ What messages did your father transmit?

   ✔ What impact did your fathers have on you?

2. After five minutes, repeat the process, but use the questions below to create lists of how they perceive the positive and negative aspects of their own fathering:

   ✔ What messages do you transmit to your children?

   ✔ What impact do you think you have on your children?

3. Distribute the worksheet and allow participants ten minutes to use the lists they generate in *Steps 1* and *2* to complete it.

4. Form groups of six and use the following questions to discuss any insights they gained while filling out the worksheets:

✔ How similar are your fathering skills to your father's?

✔ How different are they?

✔ How effective was your father?

✔ How effective are you?

✔ What specific aspects of your fathering would you like to change?

5. After thirty minutes, reconvene the entire group and allow each participant five minutes to write a contract to himself on how he is going to consciously try to alter his style of fathering.

   ☞ *Make sure participants know they will read their contract worksheets to the group.*

6. Close by having each participant read his contract to the entire group and allow time for the group members to develop ideas to help each other stick to their contracts.

This design is an adaptation of work by Glen Gaumnitz and Michael Nord.

FATHERING CHARACTERISTICS

As a father, I do these things well, just as my father did.	As a father, I do these things poorly, just as my father did.
As a father, I do these things better than my father did.	As a father, I do these things worse than my father did.

37 I, ROLE MODEL

Using brainstorming sessions and worksheets, participants explore the importance of being a positive role model to their kids and examine their own behavior as role models.

GOALS

To examine our roles and the values we pass on to our children.

To decide if we want to change our behavior as role models.

TIME

1–1½ hours.

GROUP SIZE

6–24 participants.

MATERIALS

Newsprint; markers; tape; pens or pencils; **I, Role Model** worksheets.

PROCESS

1. Invite each participant to think back to his childhood and to yell out phrases he remembers being directed at him when he was a child or teenager, record them on newsprint, and discuss them.

   ☞ *It might help to generate ideas if you ask them to think of "commands" that began with "Don't. . . ." or "Always. . . ."*

2. Lead a brainstorming session to create a list of the people in participants' lives who influenced them during various stages of their youth.

3. Verify their list with a chalktalk based on the following points:

   • As our lists indicate, it is not always clear what we mean when we talk about role models. Let's look at some basic values we pass on as role models to our children:

     ○ Values about work

     ○ Values about money

     ○ Values about intimacy and touching

     ○ Values about prejudice

©1995 Whole Person Press 210 W Michigan Duluth MN 55802   (800) 247-6789

○ Values about honesty

○ Values about drugs and alcohol

○ Values about violence

○ Values about parenting

● Your children look to you as a role model for these basic values and, just as important, they learn from you how to put values into action.

● Whether you like it or not, you are their primary role model during the early years from infancy to puberty.

● Peers and other important adults such as teachers gradually serve as additional role models, but your children continue to model themselves after you and your spouse.

4. Distribute the worksheet and allow about fifteen minutes for participants to complete the open-ended sentences.

5. Have participants share their statements with the entire group, and then conduct a brief discussion about common and unique replies.

☞ *It usually works best to have everyone respond to one question and then move on, saving the discussion until each has had a turn.*

6. Conclude the exercise by asking each man to complete one more open-ended sentence:

● I learned that when I am around my kids, I . . .

VARIATION

■ To provide food for thought you may wish to open or close the exercise by playing Harry Chapin's "Cat's in the Cradle "or another song with appropriate lyrics . ("Cat's in the Cradle" is available on *Harry Chapin: Anthology* [cassette] or *Harry Chapin: Gold Medal Collection* [CD]. Both are distributed by Electra Record).

I, ROLE MODEL

Please complete the following open-ended statements:

1. When I hug my wife in front of my kids, I feel . . .

2. When I hug my kids, I feel . . .

3. I show the most vulnerability around my kids when . . .

4. If I feel like crying around my kids I . . .

5. If I were to cry in front of my children they would . . .

6. My kids see me as successful when . . .

7. I see myself as successful when . . .

8. When my kids see me doing housework, I feel . . .

I, ROLE MODEL, continued

9. I teach my kids about work when . . .

10. I show my sexuality around my children by . . .

11. If I found my son or daughter masturbating, I . . .

12. If my son or daughter found me with a woman other than my wife, I would . . .

    They would . . .

13. The one thing I want to do more with my kids is . . .

14. When I am angry around my kids, I . . .

15. The role model I set for my kids is . . .

16. The one thing I want to change about the role model I portray is . . .

38 SUPER-DAD

Participants use a labelling activity to compare the expectations placed on them by society and family with their personal needs and to examine the problems that arise when expectations and needs conflict.

GOALS

To understand some of the typical expectations of fathers and how we deal with them.

To identify conflicts between expectations of others and our own personal needs.

To explore methods of resolving such conflicts.

TIME

1–1½ hours.

GROUP SIZE

6–24 participants.

MATERIALS

Newsprint; markers; tape; pens or pencils; **Fatherly Expectations** worksheet.

PROCESS

1. Distribute the worksheet and allow participants five to ten minutes to complete it.

2. On newsprint, draw a large outline like the one on the worksheet and have the entire group contribute their labels to this "Super-Dad."

3. Provide the instructions below and allow ten minutes for participants to follow them:

   ➤ Turn over your worksheets and draw a line that divides the page in half vertically.

   ➤ Consider all the expectations of "Super-Dad" and write those you experience most on the left-hand side of the page.

   ➤ On the right-hand side, write down a corresponding personal need you have that conflicts with each expectation.

4. Form small groups and have each participant take a turn sharing one conflict, then have the groups brainstorm ways of dealing with each participant's conflict.

5. Reconvene the entire group to share innovative resolutions.

VARIATION

■ For a fun closing activity, present the "Super-est Dad" award to the member with the most creative conflict-resolution ideas.

FATHERLY EXPECTATIONS

Directions: Label the body drawing with titles that express expectations our society places on fathers. For example, you might label "handyman" next to one of the hands or "caring" next to the heart. Be as creative as possible: the more labels, the better.

39 ROLES WE CAST OUR CHILDREN IN

As a way of becoming more aware of the pressures they place on their kids, participants examine how they perceive their children and themselves.

GOALS

To become more aware of how we perceive our children and ourselves.

To create a greater awareness of how people cast their family members in certain roles.

To become more aware of the anxieties casting our children in roles can cause.

TIME

1 hour.

GROUP SIZE

6–24 participants.

MATERIALS

Pens or pencils; **Roles for Self & Child** worksheets.

PROCESS

1. Introduce the exercise and its goals with a chalktalk based on the following points:

   - It is human nature to cast our family members into certain roles.
   - Some of these roles are positive, others negative.
   - Regardless of what types of roles we cast our family members in, the roles tend to freeze the type of behaviors we see in them.
   - For example, we may think of one of our kids as athletic and encourage him or her to participate in sports, sometimes closing them off to other activities.
   - Such a "freezing" process creates anxiety in each family member over possible unfulfilled expectations.
   - This makes it difficult for family members to step outside of their preconceived roles and experience full self-expression.

● In this exercise, we're going to focus on becoming more aware of the
  roles we cast our children in as well as how we perceive ourselves.

2. Distribute the worksheet and allow participants about ten minutes to
   complete it.

3. Have participants examine their worksheets and place a star by the five
   words that best describe themselves and underline the five that best
   describe their children.

4. Form small groups and use the following questions to discuss the
   worksheets:

   ✔ Are the top five roles you assigned your child similar to those you
     gave yourself?

   ✔ How many of those top five did you assign to both you and your
     child?

   ✔ How do the adjectives and nouns on the list lock people into roles?

   ✔ How have the expectations of the roles you have assigned your kids
     made them act or react?

   ✔ How can family members break out of these roles?

5. Reconvene the entire group and lead a brainstorming session to create
   ways of learning not to assign roles.

VARIATIONS

■ If time allows, let participants fill out a worksheet for each of their
  children.

This exercise was developed by Rae and Howard Millman of Columbia, Maryland.

©1995 Whole Person Press 210 W Michigan Duluth MN 55802   (800) 247-6789

ROLES FOR SELF & CHILD

Directions: Write your name under "Self"; write the name of one of your children under "Child." For each pair of descriptive words on the left, choose the word that comes closest to fitting yourself and your child. Force yourself to pick one from each pair. You may pick the same one for each or a different one for each of you.

	Self	Child
1. Serious / Clown		
2. Active / Inactive		
3. Smart / Average		
4. Participant / Spectator		
5. Healthy / Sickly		
6. Truthful / Dishonest		
7. Athletic / Unathletic		
8. Strong / Weak		
9. Helpful / Unhelpful		
10. Studious / Not studious		
11. Open / Closed		
12. Nervous / Calm		
13. Optimistic / Pessimistic		
14. Sure-footed / Clumsy		

ROLES FOR SELF & CHILD, continued

	Self	Child
15. Talkative / Quiet		
16. Modest / Immodest		
17. Confident / Embarrassed		
18. Questioner / Answerer		
19. Leader / Follower		
20. Loyal / Disloyal		
21. Responsible / Irresponsible		
22. Aggressive / Passive		
23. Rugged / Prissy		
24. Prince / Princess		
25. Whiner / Stoic		
26. Bully / Patsy		
27. Blamer / Martyr		
28. Pest / Joy		
29. Easy / Difficult		
30. Friendly / Unfriendly		

40 PREGNANT FATHERS

Designed specifically for fathers-to-be, this exercise allows participants to discuss their hopes and fears of becoming a father and helps prepare them for inevitable changes in their life-style.

GOALS

To understand feelings surrounding impending fatherhood.

To plan for the life-style adjustments of becoming a father.

TIME

1 1/2–2 hours.

GROUP SIZE

6–24 participants.

MATERIALS

Newsprint; markers; tape.

PROCESS

1. Introduce the exercise and have participants find a comfortable place to relax. Then ask them to silently consider the following questions:

   ✔ When did you first learn about your coming child?

   ✔ Who told you?

   ✔ Where were you?

   ✔ What did you feel?

   ✔ Who did you want to tell?

   ✔ Who did you actually tell first and when?

2. After five minutes, form two groups, one consisting of participants who already have children and another of those who will become fathers for the first time. Have the groups sit opposite one another. Then have the first group share their reactions to the questions in *Step 1*.

   ☞ *If you have a large group, you will want to monitor time and keep things moving. Try not to use up more than ten minutes each for Steps 2 and 3.*

3. Reverse *Step 2*; the first-time-fathers-to-be discuss their reactions while the other group observes.

   ☞ *Record a list of the common feelings and reactions of each group.*

4. Use the lists generated in *Steps 2* and *3* to lead a discussion between the two groups, noting similarities and differences.

5. Form groups of four, making sure to mix together members of the previous groups, and have participants spend twenty minutes discussing how their attitudes toward their partner have changed since her pregnancy began.

6. Reconvene the entire group and have each small group report the highlights of their discussion.

7. Reform the small groups and ask participants to use the following questions to discuss their anticipated life-style changes:

   ✔ How are you preparing for the birth?

   ✔ What basic changes are you anticipating?

   ✔ Are you adjusting your finances in any way?

   ✔ Current fathers, what changes that you did not anticipate occurred after your first child was born?

   ✔ What steps are you taking to help support your wife?

8. After thirty minutes, reconvene the entire group and have each small group report their response to the questions in *Step 7*, record them on newsprint, and brainstorm any more ideas that will help participants prepare for this major life change.

9. Close by having each participant complete the following open-ended sentence:

   • I want to give my wife and my child . . .

41 WHAT DO I GET FOR MY MONEY?

This exercise helps fathers that do not live with their children full time explore their feelings and expectations about parenting and the frustration that often accompanies paying child support.

GOALS

To gain more insight into our feelings about not being with our children as often as we would like when we help pay to support them.

To understand our expectations and desires about fathering children when we are separated from them.

TIME

1–1½ hours.

GROUP SIZE

6–12 participants.

MATERIALS

Newsprint; markers; tape.

PROCESS

1. Invite participants to introduce themselves by briefly stating their feelings about being apart from their children.

2. Next, ask each to share his feelings about child support by answering the following question:

   ✔ What is the difference between supporting your kids financially and paying support for your kids?

3. Form groups of three and have participants spend about twenty minutes using the following questions to discuss their feelings about child support:

   ✔ When do I find myself angry about paying support?

   ✔ How have I used child support in arguments?

   ✔ Have I used child support to threaten my former partner?

   ✔ How does my attitude about child support affect my kids?

4. Ask the groups to share what each sees as the greatest problem involved in child support and help each other create solutions to these conflicts. Focus on the following:

    ✔ How much am I giving?

    ✔ What do I want to be giving?

    ✔ What do I expect as a result of this?

    ✔ What do I get in return?

5. After twenty minutes, reconvene the entire group and have each trio share their problems and solutions and, as a large group, brainstorm creative ways to overcoming the problems caused and issues raised by child support.

©1995 Whole Person Press 210 W Michigan Duluth MN 55802   (800) 247-6789

42 FATHERING: SEPARATED CHILDREN

This second exercise for fathers separated from their children focuses on personal feelings about being a good parent when they can only be with their children part time.

GOALS

To understand some of the personal issues involved with having our children with us only part-time.

To clarify our values in respect to our children.

TIME

1–1½ hours.

GROUP SIZE

6–12 participants.

MATERIALS

Newsprint; markers; tape.

PROCESS

1. Invite each participant to introduce himself and reflect on his feelings about fathering separated children. Ask each to include the following:

   • How many children he has.

   • A description of each child (age, physical appearance, personality, interests, etc.)

   • How often they see them.

   • How they feel when their children are with them and when they are apart.

   ☞ Record their feelings on newsprint for later in the exercise.

2. Form small groups and allow ten minutes for participants to discuss the feelings they mentioned in their introductions; in particular, have them attempt to identify the roots of their concerns.

3. Reconvene the entire group and ask for volunteers to role-play one of their own children. Have each volunteer do a monologue, as if they were one of their children, describing what typically happens at Dad's house:

what it is like, what they do, who else is there, what they like or don't like about the situation, etc.

4. After the volunteers have finished, ask all the participants to share their reactions in order to better understand what their children might feel when they are with them.

   ☞ *Post responses on newsprint.*

5. Compare and discuss the lists generated in *Steps 1* and *4*, noting significant similarities and differences, and explore what fathers can do to resolve conflicts and increase the quality of the time they spend with their children.

6. Close the session by having each participant state at least one thing they will do differently during the next visit with their children.

43 FATHERING: STEPCHILDREN

Using word association techniques, this exercise provides an opportunity for fathers with stepchildren to explore the unique issues surrounding parenting the children of others and develop ways to handle special concerns.

GOALS

To understand some of the issues particular to having stepchildren.

To create ways to handle the pressures of stepfather/child relationships.

TIME

1–1½ hours.

GROUP SIZE

6–12 participants.

MATERIALS

Newsprint; markers; tape.

PROCESS

1. Explain the objectives and introduce the exercise by leading participants in a brainstorming session to create a list of nouns and adjectives
   associated with the word "stepfather."

   ☞ *Record the responses on newsprint and explore briefly any terms
   which do not seem clear or that participants want to know more
   about.*

2. Tape two pieces of newsprint on a wall, one labelled "Joys of having
   stepchildren" and the other "Pains of having stepchildren," and have
   each participant provide one or two items to add to each list.

   ☞ *Allow enough space between the two sheets to place a third.*

3. Form small groups and allow them about fifteen minutes to discuss the
   "Joys" and "Pains" lists using the following questions:

   ✔ What particular instances make you think of an item on the
   "Joys" list?

   ✔ How do you feel when you experience an item on the "Joys" list?

✔ What particular instances make you think of an item on the "Pains" list?

✔ How do you feel when you experience an item on the "Pains" list?

☞ *Ask them to try to avoid problem-solving at this point.*

4. Tape another newsprint between the "Joys" and "Pains" sheets, title it "Bridges," and have the small groups spend fifteen minutes discussing ways they celebrate the joys, deal with the pains, and build bridges from bad experiences to good.

5. Reconvene the entire group and have each small group share their most useful and creative "bridges."

☞ *Record this information on the "Bridges" sheet.*

6. Close by having participants complete the following open-ended sentences:

- Today I learned . . .

- The next time I have a conflict with a stepchild, I will . . .

VARIATION

■ If appropriate to the group, have participants compare feelings they have about their stepchildren to those they have about their biological children. Compare similarities and differences.

■ This design can also be used quite fruitfully with couples who have stepchildren.

PARENTING READING LIST

Block, Joyce. *Family Myths: Living Out Roles, Betraying Ourselves*. New York: Simon and Schuster, 1994.

Buscaglia, Leo. *Papa, My Father*. New York: William Morrow & Co, 1989.

Colman, Arthur and Libby Colman. *The Father: Mythology and Changing Roles*. Chicago: Chiron Publications, 1988.

Cosby, Bill. *Childhood*. New York: G. P. Putnam's Sons, 1991.

Coulter, Barbara and Joan Minninger, Ph.D. *The Father-Daughter Dance*. New York: G.P. Putnam's Sons, 1993.

Epstein, Rick. *Rookie Dad*. New York: Hypersion Press, 1992.

Greif, Geoffrey L. *The Daddy Track and The Single Father*. Lexington, Mass.: Lexington Books, 1990.

Hutchinson, Earl, Ph.D. *Black Fatherhood: The Guide to Male Parenting*. Los Angeles: Impact Publications, 1992.

Kivel, Paul. *Men's Work*. New York: Ballantine Books, 1992.

Osherson, Samuel, Ph.D. *Finding Our Fathers: How a Man's Life Is Shaped by the Relationship with His Father*. New York: Fawcett, 1988.

Samuels, Andrew. Editor of *The Father: Contemporary Jungian Perspectives*. New York: New York University Press, 1985.

Shapiro, Jerold Lee, Ph.D. *The Measure of a Man: Becoming the Father You Wish Your Father Had Been*. New York: Delaconte Press, 1993.

Resources
for Men

RESOURCES FOR MEN

There is a growing list of men's groups around the country. Some deal with single issue areas such as "divorced fathers" or "legal aid for men." Others serve as centering points in their respective communities for men in search of personal growth. Regardless of what they were established for, the list below, which is by no means complete, reflects the growing interest in men in their own well-being. There has been a great deal of fluidity in the men's movement over the last fifteen years, so some groups may not exist or have transformed themselves somewhat. Local universities or community colleges are also an excellent place to seek out local resources. This resource list is divided into two areas:

1. Specialized Groups
2. Regional Support Groups

SPECIALIZED GROUPS

Single Dad's Life-style
Phoenix Rising
P.O. Box 484Z
Scottsdale, AZ 85258

National Council on Marriage &
Divorce Law Reform Orgs.
P.O. Box 60
Broomall, PA 19008

Men Against Patriarchy
4811 Springfield Avenue
Philadelphia, PA 19143

Men's Advisory Committee
The Counseling Center
of Milwaukee
1428 North Farrell Avenue
Milwaukee, WI 53202

Fathers United for Equal Rights
P.O. Box 11243
Baltimore, MD 21239

Equal Rights On Divorce, Inc.
P.O. Box 211
Clarksburg, MD 20734

REGIONAL SUPPORT GROUPS

Many of these groups tend to be located on college campuses.

National Men's Resource Center
P.O. Box 800
San Anselmo, CA 94979

Los Angeles Men's Collective
6286 Commodore Sloat Drive
Los Angeles, CA 90048

Men's Awareness
Network of Summit
P.O. Box 483
Summit, NJ 07901

Men's Center
P.O. Box 14299
University Station
Minneapolis, MN 55414

Male Awareness Center
P.O. Box 66123
Houston, TX 77006

The Male's Place
976 Lonzen Avenue
San Jose, CA 95126

Mankind Marin
P.O. Box 1392
San Rafael, CA 94902

Men's Center
Harold Wells
2718 University
Des Moines, IA 50311

Boston Men's Center
Campus Free College
Boston, MA 02108

Men's Center
235 Wayne Street
Highland Park, NJ 08904

Knoxville Men's
Resource Collective
P.O. Box 8060 UT Station
Knoxville, TN 37916

Men's Equality Now International
One West 6th Street
Wilmington, DE 19801

Men's Center JFK Lobby
Southwest Residential College
University of Massachusetts
Amherst, MA 01003

New Men's Center
Francis W. Barrow
2140 South Glenwood
Springfield, IL 62704

Men's Resource Center
909 4th Avenue
Seattle, WA 98104

Austin Men's Center
700 West Avenue
Austin, TX 78701

Men's Resource Center
3534 SE Main
Portland, Oregon 97214

Washington Area Men's
Awareness Network
P.0. Box 21026
Washington, D.C. 20009

East Bay Men's Center
2700 Bancroft Way
Berkeley, CA 94704

Denver Area Men's Network
2323 Dahlia
Denver, CO 80207

Basic Education Project
Men's Center
P.O. Box 1025
Ann Arbor, MI 48106

The Malebox
P.O. Box 8113
Ann Arbor, MI 48107

Men's Resource Center
909 4th Avenue
Seattle, WA 98104

Men's Center of New York
257 Seventh Avenue
New York, NY 10001

Men's Task Force
P.O. Box 5064
Champaign, IL 61820

Turning Point
University YMCA
306 North Brooks Street
Madison, WI 53715

Oberlin Men's Center
Box 893 Oberlin College
Oberlin, OH 44074

Olympia Men's Collective
P.O. Box 2811
Olympia, WA 98507

Project Redirection
15770 Heyden
Detroit, MI 48227

St. Louis Men's Projects
P.O. Box 8157
St. Louis, MO 63108

San Francisco Men's Center
P.O. Box 6072
San Francisco, CA 94120

Cincinnati Men's Network
David Jaggar
3618 Middleton Avenue
Cincinnati, OH 45220

Seattle Men
602 W Howe Street
Seattle, WA 98119

Earth Men Resources
P.O. Box 1034
Evanston, IL 60204

Chesapeake Men's Council
(703) 522-9876

Baltimore Men's Council
(410) 467-1713

A good source for finding men's groups in the northeast is:

Resources for Men Northeast: A Directory of 148 Men's Groups by B. Peterson. Available from New Views Educational Services, Inc., P.O. Box 137, Little Ferry, NJ 07643.

How to Use This Book
Most Effectively

THE CONCEPT OF EXPERIENTIAL LEARNING

As you will notice with just a cursory glance through this volume, these educational experiences actively involve participants in the learning process. Why? Because when you draw on the resources of the group in your presentations, you empower people.

Every session in this book balances didactic information and group participation. Experiential training concentrates on developing awareness and understanding plus building skills that can be used at home and on the job. This model helps participants become involved and therefore makes it more likely they will assume responsibility for their own learning.

Each exercise is designed to create opportunities for participants to interact with the concepts and each other in meaningful ways. The lecture method is replaced with succinct chalktalks and facilitative questions that guide people to discover their own answers. The authority of the trainer is transformed into the authority of the individual's inner wisdom.

THE TRAINER'S CHALLENGE

For many teachers, giving up the authority implicit in the typical lecture format is a risky proposition. Trainers are often afraid that they won't be perceived as an expert, so they are tempted to lecture, entertain and keep the focus on themselves. Yet, if your goal is truly to help people change, information is not enough. Praise from your audience is not enough. What really counts are the discoveries participants make about their own patterns and the choices they make to manage their lives more effectively.

Remember, as a trainer, you are not presenting a paper at a conference. You are engaging an audience in an educational process. Your task is to appeal to people with different learning styles, using a wide variety of strategies to get them involved. In whole person learning, the questions are as important as the content.

THE TEACHING STRATEGIES

These exercises help you involve people in the process of reflecting, prioritizing, sorting, and planning for change by using the following strategies.

1. **Activating participants' internal wisdom**: This is best accomplished by asking questions that help people come up with answers that are right for them, rather than by giving them your "right answers."

2. **Helping people make choices**: These exercises assist people to sort out their own values and priorities, helping them to explore their beliefs and assumptions and encouraging them to alter their lives in ways that they choose, based on their own sense of rhythm and timing.

3. **Activating the group's resources**: These exercises take the dynamic of the group seriously. The first five minutes are the key! They help you get people involved with each other right off the bat, and let you use and work with the energy of the group—the laughter, the group norms, the embarrassment, the competition.

4. **Fostering interpersonal support**: With these exercises you capitalize on the rich variety of experiences and insights among your participants. And you capitalize on the power of their support for each other. Interaction builds trust, helps people consider new options, and offers support for change. For many people this chance to compare notes with others is the most powerful part of the session.

THE RHYTHM OF EACH SESSION

To accomplish these teaching objectives each exercise is designed to include a rhythmic sequence of activities with enough change of pace to keep the group's involvement and energy high. Most exercises include:

A warm-up—An introductory activity that gets people involved with each other around the subject in an energetic and playful manner.

A chalktalk—A brief introduction to the session's main concepts.

Personal reflection—Questions to help each participant test the concepts against their own life experiences in order to determine which ideas make sense to them.

Inductive summary—A pooling of the group's observations and insights.

Planning/commitment—The bottom line in training. Everyone should leave the session with a commitment to think over the new ideas that were generated in the discussion and a willingness to consider making changes in their life.

THE FORMAT

The format of this book is designed for easy use. Every exercise is described completely, including goals, group size, time, materials needed, step-by-step process instructions, and variations. The format employs the following symbols to help indicate specific items:

©1995 Whole Person Press 210 W Michigan Duluth MN 55802   (800) 247-6789

☞ *Special instructions for the trainer are set in italics and preceded by a pointing hand.*

✔ Questions to ask participants are preceded by a check.

➤ Instructions for group activities are indicated by an arrow.

• Chalktalk (mini-lecture) notes and sentence-completion fragments are preceded by a bullet.

Time: The time frame provided at the beginning of each exercise and times given for various activities within the process are only guidelines— suggestions to help you organize and schedule a successful workshop. Feel free to adapt the times as you feel necessary.

Worksheets: Many of the exercises include worksheets for participants to complete. The worksheets can be found immediately following the exercises in which they are to be used. Make certain you photocopy enough worksheets for all your participants prior to conducting an exercise. (8 1/2" x 11" photocopy masters for this book are also available from Whole Person Associates.)

Chalktalks: Most of the exercises include chalktalk notes—bulleted lists of information that help introduce an exercise or provide vital information on its topic. These notes provide a framework to help you develop a complete mini-lecture of your own.

TIPS FOR USING THESE EXERCISES MOST EFFECTIVELY

1. **Tailor your process to the group**: Read the objectives for each exercise and carefully choose those you will use. Remember, these exercises are more than fun and games. Each one has a clear purpose.

   Decide what is appropriate based on the setting, the time available, the purpose and the participants' style and comfort level. Exercises should be specifically selected for a particular organization and should be tailored to that organization's style and culture. What will work well in one situation may not work as effectively in another. Feel free to adapt exercises as you deem necessary.

2. **Pay attention to the timing**: In your planning, anticipate the needs and rhythm of the group. At the first session you'll need more time for setting the ground rules and getting acquainted. In later sessions, as people get to know each other better you'll need to allocate more time for the discussion segments.

Every group goes through predictable (and unpredictable!) cycles. Anticipate peak times and down times during the day and plan for changing the pace as needed to restore energy and enthusiasm.

3. **Prepare yourself thoroughly for each session**: Good training is built on examples and anecdotes. In order to make the material come alive for you and for others, you will need to carefully work through each session and personalize each segment with your own examples and stories. You can do this in a number of ways:

   • Read the detailed exercise outline thoroughly. Be sure you understand the basic concepts and processes for the session. Answer all worksheet questions for yourself. This will help you anticipate difficulties and will provide you with lively personal examples.

   • Reread the chalktalk notes one point at a time. Translate the ideas into your own words. Personalize each concept with carefully chosen examples that you think will fit the group's needs.

   • It is often helpful to work with another person. If you are sharing the tasks of facilitation, be sure to decide how you will work together.

   • Add diagrams, cartoons, newspaper articles—whatever relevant information you come across during your preparation.

   • Relax. Take a few minutes by yourself before you begin each session so that you are centered and focused.

4. **Make the environment work for you**: The room makes a very important contribution to the atmosphere. The best location has soft lighting, comfortable chairs, is neither too big nor too small, and has privacy to prevent interruptions that would distract the group. If you must meet in a room that's too large, keep the group together. Don't let people spread out all over—distance breeds isolation.

   Banked auditoriums with fixed seats are workable, but not recommended. The inflexibility of the seating makes movement exercises and small group gatherings more difficult.

   Encourage participants to sit in a circle. This creates the most successful setting since it provides an ideal forum for verbal and nonverbal communication and offers an atmosphere of inclusion.

   You will want to have a chalkboard or sheets of newsprint (or both!) available for your use at all times.

   Don't expect anyone else to set up the room for you. Get there early and if necessary, set it up yourself.

5. Establish a supportive atmosphere: Participants in your sessions must feel safe enough to examine their attitudes and beliefs and to change some of them. A trainer open to listening to what all participants say creates an atmosphere of security.

Always restate a participant's comment or question before you respond. Summarizing what you heard affirms the person and shows your audience that you are listening and taking them seriously.

Begin the workshop with a discussion of guidelines for the session. This helps alleviate anxiety and sets a positive tone. Suggestions include: attend regularly and be on time, listen to each other carefully, and respect confidentiality.

6. Carefully plan the small group discussions: For most discussions, groups of four to six are optimal. Timing will be a problem if some groups have three people and others have eight. So try to keep groups the same size as indicated in the instructions.

In many exercises your leader notes tell you how to divide the participants into small groups. In others the "how to" is left up to you.

If some people don't participate (or even leave the room during group sharing time) don't panic. Don't drop the group experience because a few people feel uncomfortable. For many people the small group discussions are the most valuable part of the session.

7. Grow from this experience yourself: Try to learn the most you can from every event. Don't be afraid to share yourself. You are a leader/participant! Don't be discouraged if each session does not go exactly as you had expected. Turn disasters into opportunities. When something does not go well, laugh! When all else fails, start asking questions.

Plan to have fun! The processes in these exercises are designed so that you have a chance to listen as well as talk. The whole experience does not depend on you. Open your eyes and your ears, you'll learn something too!

Whole Person Associates Resources

All printed, audio, and video resources developed by Whole Person Associates are designed to address the whole person—physical, emotional, mental, spiritual, and social. On the next pages, trainers will find a wide array of resources that offer ready-to-use ideas and concepts they can add to their programs.

GROUP PROCESS RESOURCES

All of the exercises in these group process resources encourage interaction between the leader and participants, as well as among the participants. Each exercise includes everything needed to present a meaningful program.

WORKING WITH WOMEN'S GROUPS
Volumes 1 & 2

Louise Yolton Eberhardt

The two volumes of **Working with Women's Groups** have been completely revised and updated. **Volume 1** explores consciousness raising, self-discovery, and assertiveness training. **Volume 2** looks at sexuality issues, women of color, and leadership skills training.

❑ **Working with Women's Groups**
   Volumes 1 & 2 / $24.95 per volume

WORKING WITH MEN'S GROUPS

Roger Karsk and Bill Thomas

Working with Men's Groups has been updated to reflect the reality of men's lives in the 1990s. Each exercise follows a structured pattern to help trainers develop either one-time workshops or ongoing groups that explore men's issues in four key areas: self-discovery, consciousness raising, intimacy, and parenting.

❑ **Working with Men's Groups / $24.95**

WORKSHEET MASTERS

Complete packages of (8 1/2" x 11") photocopy masters are available for **Working with Women's Groups** and **Working with Men's Groups**. Use the masters to conveniently duplicate handouts for each participant.

❑ **Worksheet Masters / $9.95 per volume**

To order, call toll free   (800) 247-6789

WORKING WITH GROUPS IN THE WORKPLACE

This new collection addresses the special needs and concerns of trainers in the workplace. As the work force changes, EAP counselors, education departments, and management are being called on to guide and support their employees who face the challenges of a more diverse workplace.

BRIDGING THE GENDER GAP
Louise Yolton Eberhardt

Bridging the Gender Gap contains a wealth of exercises for the trainer to use with men and women who work as colleagues. These activities will also be useful in gender role awareness groups, diversity training, couples workshops, college classes, and youth seminars.

❑ **Bridging the Gender Gap / $24.95**

CONFRONTING SEXUAL HARASSMENT
Louise Yolton Eberhardt

Confronting Sexual Harassment presents exercises that trainers can safely use with groups to constructively explore the issues of sexual harassment, look at the underlying causes, understand the law, motivate men to become allies, and empower women to speak up.

❑ **Confronting Sexual Harassment / $24.95**

CELEBRATING DIVERSITY
Cheryl Hetherington

Celebrating Diversity helps people confront and question the beliefs, prejudices, and fears that can separate them from others. Carefully written exercises help trainers present these sensitive issues in the workplace as well as in educational settings.

❑ **Celebrating Diversity / $24.95**

WORKSHEET MASTERS
Complete packages of (8 1/2" x 11") photocopy masters are available for all books in the **Working with Groups in the Workplace** series.

❑ **Worksheet Masters / $9.95 per volume**

To order, call toll free   (800) 247-6789

STRESS AND WELLNESS ANNOTATED GUIDES

From worksite health promotion to life-style research to family stress, these authoritative reviews of classic and contemporary information sources will help you locate the resources you need for planning workshops, classes, program proposals, or presentations on stress and wellness.

STRESS RESOURCES
An annotated guide to essential books, periodicals, A-V materials and teaching tools about stress for trainers, consultants, counselors, educators and health professionals
Selected and reviewed by Jim Polidora, Ph.D.

Jim Polidora reviews the best current and classic, popular and scientific literature in every area of stress management. Over 500 annotations are arranged topically for easy reference.

Each of the fifteen chapters includes reviews of books and audiovisual resources. Special sections feature textbooks, catalogs, journals, newsletters, and stress-related organizations.

❑ **Stress Resources / $34.95**

WELLNESS RESOURCES
An annotated guide to essential books, periodicals, A-V materials and teaching tools about wellness for trainers, consultants, counselors, educators and health professionals
Selected and reviewed by Jim Polidora, Ph.D.

This first comprehensive guide to wellness resources is packed with descriptions of over 500 of the best current and classic books, audiotapes, videotapes, journals, newsletters, and catalogs.

The fifteen chapters of reading and viewing suggestions in **Wellness Resources** make workshop or program planning a breeze.

❑ **Wellness Resources / $34.95**

To order, call toll free   (800) 247-6789

STRUCTURED EXERCISES IN STRESS MANAGEMENT

Nancy Loving Tubesing, EdD, and Donald A. Tubesing, PhD, Editors

Each book in this four-volume series contains 36 ready-to-use teaching modules that involve the participant—as a whole person—in learning how to manage stress more effectively.

Each volume brims with practical ideas that mix and match allowing trainers to develop new programs for varied settings, audiences, and time frames. Each volume contains **Icebreakers, Stress Assessments, Management Strategies, Skill Builders, Action Planners, Closing Processes,** and **Group Energizers**.

- ❏ **Stress 8 1/2" x 11" Loose-Leaf Edition—Volume 1-4 / $54.95 each**
- ❏ **Stress 6" x 9" Softcover Edition—Volume 1-4 / $29.95 each**

STRUCTURED EXERCISES IN WELLNESS PROMOTION

Nancy Loving Tubesing, EdD, and Donald A. Tubesing, PhD, Editors

Each of the four volumes in this innovative series includes 36 experiential learning activities that focus on whole person health—body, mind, spirit, emotions, relationships, and life-style.

Icebreakers, Wellness Explorations, Self-Care Strategies, Action Planners, Closings, and **Group Energizers** are all ready-to-go—including reproducible worksheets, scripts, and chalktalk outlines—for the busy professional who wants to develop unique wellness programs without spending hours in preparation.

- ❏ **Wellness 8 1/2" x 11" Loose-Leaf Edition—Volume 1-4 / $54.95 each**
- ❏ **Wellness 6" x 9" Softcover Edition—Volume 1-4 / $29.95 each**

WORKSHEET MASTERS

Complete packages of (8 1/2" x 11") photocopy masters are available for all **Structured Exercises in Stress Management** and **Structured Exercises in Wellness Promotion**. Use the masters to conveniently duplicate handouts for each participant.

- ❏ **Worksheet Masters / $9.95 per volume**

To order, call toll free   (800) 247-6789

RELAXATION AUDIOTAPES

Perhaps you're an old hand at relaxation, looking for new ideas. Or maybe you're a beginner, just testing the waters. Whatever your relaxation needs, Whole Person audiotapes provide a whole family of options for reducing physical and mental stress.

Techniques range from simple breathing and stretching exercises to classic autogenic and progressive relaxation sequences, guided meditations, and whimsical daydreams. All are carefully crafted to promote whole person relaxation—body, mind, and spirit.

If you're looking for an extended relaxation experience (20 minutes or more), try a tape from the Sensational Relaxation, Guided Imagery, or Wilderness Daydreams groups. For quick R&R breaks (5–10 minutes), try a Stress Breaks, Daydreams or Mini-Meditations collections. All of our tapes feature male and female narrators.

Audiotapes are available for $11.95 each.
Call for generous quantity discounts.

SENSATIONAL RELAXATION—$11.95 each
When stress piles up, it becomes a heavy load both physically and emotionally. These full-length relaxation experiences will teach you techniques that can be used whenever you feel that stress is getting out of control. Choose one you like and repeat it daily until it becomes second nature, then recall that technique whenever you need it or try a new one every day.

- ❏ **Countdown to Relaxation /** Countdown 19:00, Staircase 19:00
- ❏ **Daybreak / Sundown /** Daybreak 22:00, Sundown 22:00
- ❏ **Take a Deep Breath /** Breathing for Relaxation 17:00, Magic Ball 17:00
- ❏ **Relax . . . Let Go . . . Relax /** Revitalization 27:00, Relaxation 28:00
- ❏ **StressRelease /** Quick Tension Relievers 22:00, Progressive Relaxation 20:00
- ❏ **Warm and Heavy /** Warm 24:00, Heavy 23:00

STRESS BREAKS—$11.95 each
Do you need a short energy booster or a quick stress reliever? If you don't know what type of relaxation you like, or if you are new to guided relaxation techniques, try one of our Stress Breaks for a quick refocusing or change of pace any time of the day.

- ❏ **BreakTime /** Solar Power 8:00, Belly Breathing 9:00, Fortune Cookie 9:00, Mother Earth 11:00, Big Yawn 5:00, Affirmation 11:00
- ❏ **Natural Tranquilizers /** Clear the Deck 10:00, Body Scan 10:00, 99 Countdown 10:00, Calm Down 9:00, Soothing Colors 11:00, Breathe Ten 9:00

To order, call toll free   (800) 247-6789

DAYDREAMS—$11.95 each

Escape from the stress around you with guided tours to beautiful places. The quick escapes in our Daydreams tapes will lead your imagination away from your everyday cares so you can resume your tasks relaxed and comforted.

- ❑ **Daydreams 1: Getaways** / Cabin Retreat 11:00, Night Sky 10:00, Hot Spring 7:00, Mountain View 8:00, Superior Sail 8:00
- ❑ **Daydreams 2: Peaceful Places** / Ocean Tides 11:00, City Park 10:00, Hammock 8:00, Meadow 11:00
- ❑ **Daydreams 3: Relaxing Retreats** / Melting Candle 5:00, Tropical Paradise 10:00, Sanctuary 7:00, Floating Clouds 5:00, Seasons 9:00, Beach Tides 9:00

GUIDED MEDITATION—$11.95 each

Take a step beyond relaxation. The imagery in our full-length meditations will help you discover your strengths, find healing, make positive life changes, and recognize your inner wisdom.

- ❑ **Inner Healing** / Inner Healing 20:00, Peace with Pain 20:00
- ❑ **Personal Empowering** / My Gifts 22:00, Hidden Strengths 21:00
- ❑ **Healthy Balancing** / Inner Harmony 20:00, Regaining Equilibrium 20:00
- ❑ **Spiritual Centering** / Spiritual Centering 20:00 (male and female narration)

WILDERNESS DAYDREAMS—$11.95 each

Discover the healing power of nature with the four tapes in our Wilderness Daydreams series. The eight special journeys will transport you from your harried, stressful surroundings to the peaceful serenity of words and water.

- ❑ **Canoe / Rain** / Canoe 19:00, Rain 22:00
- ❑ **Island / Spring** / Island 19:00, Spring 19:00
- ❑ **Campfire / Stream** / Campfire 17:00, Stream 19:00
- ❑ **Sailboat / Pond** / Sailboat 25:00, Pond 25:00

MINI-MEDITATIONS—$11.95 each

These brief guided visualizations begin by focusing your breathing and uncluttering your mind, so that you can concentrate on a sequence of sensory images that promote relaxation, centering, healing, growth, and spiritual awareness.

- ❑ **Healing Visions** / Rocking Chair 5:00, Pine Forest 8:00, Long Lost Confidant 10:00, Caterpillar to Butterfly 7:00, Superpowers 9:00, Tornado 8:00
- ❑ **Refreshing Journeys** / 1 to 10 10:00, Thoughts Library 11:00, Visualizing Change 6:00, Magic Carpet 9:00, Pond of Love 9:00, Cruise 9:00

MUSIC ONLY—$11.95 each

No relaxation program would be complete without relaxing melodies that can be played as background to a prepared script or that can be enjoyed as you practice a technique you have already learned. Steven Eckels composed his melodies specifically for relaxation. These "musical prayers for healing" will calm your body, mind, and spirit.

- ❑ **Tranquility** / Awakening 20:00, Repose 20:00
- ❑ **Harmony** / Waves of Light 30:00, Rising Mist 10:00, Frankincense 10:00, Angelica 10:00
- ❑ **Serenity** / Radiance 20:00, Quiessence 10:00, Evanesence 10:00

To order, call toll free   (800) 247-6789

RELAXATION RESOURCES

Many trainers and workshop leaders have discovered the benefits of relaxation and visualization in healing the body, mind, and spirit.

30 SCRIPTS FOR RELAXATION, IMAGERY, AND INNER HEALING
Julie Lusk

The relaxation scripts, creative visualizations and guided meditations in these volumes were created by experts in the field of guided imagery. Julie Lusk collected their best and most effective scripts to help novices get started and experienced leaders expand their repertoire. Both volumes include information on how to use the scripts, suggestions for tailoring them to specific needs and audiences, and information on how to successfully incorporate guided imagery into existing programs.

❑ 30 Scripts
  Volume 1 & 2 / $19.95 each

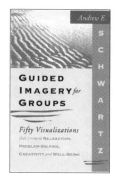

GUIDED IMAGERY FOR GROUPS
Andrew Schwartz

Ideal for courses, workshops, team building, and personal stress management, this comprehensive resource includes scripts for 50 thematic visualizations that promote calming, centering, creativity, congruence, clarity, coping, and connectedness. Detailed instructions for using relaxation techniques and guided images in group settings allow educators at all levels, in any setting, to help people tap into the healing and creative powers of imagery.

❑ Guided Imagery for Groups / $24.95

INQUIRE WITHIN
Andrew Schwartz

Use visualization to help people make positive changes in their life. The 24 visualization experiences in **Inquire Within** will help participants enhance their creativity, heal inner pain, learn to relax, and deal with conflict. Each visualization includes questions at the end of the process that encourage deeper reflection and a better understanding of the exercise and the response it evokes.

❑ Inquire Within / $19.95

To order, call toll free (800) 247-6789

PLAYFUL ACTIVITIES FOR POWERFUL PRESENTATIONS
Bruce Williamson

Spice up presentations with healthy laughter. The 40 creative energizers in *Playful Activities for Powerful Presentations* will enhance learning, stimulate communication, promote teamwork, and reduce resistance to group interaction.

This potent but light-hearted resource will make presentations on any topic more powerful and productive.

❑ Playful Activities for Powerful Presentations $19.95

WORKING WITH GROUPS FROM DYSFUNCTIONAL FAMILIES
Cheryl Hetherington

Even the healthiest family can be dysfunctional at times, making everyone vulnerable to the pain of difficult family relationships.

This collection of 29 proven group activities is designed to heal the pain that results from living in a dysfunctional family. With these exercises leaders can promote healing, build self-esteem,
encourage sharing, and help participants acknowledge their feelings.

❑ Working with Groups from Dysfunctional Families / $24.95

WORKSHEET MASTERS
A complete package of (8 1/2" x 11") photocopy masters is available for **Working with Groups from Dysfunctional Families**. Use the masters to conveniently duplicate handouts for each participant.

❑ Worksheet Masters / $9.95 per volume

To order, call toll free   (800) 247-6789

VIDEO RESOURCES

These video-based workshops use the power of professionally produced videotapes as a starting point. Then they build on the experience with printed guides chock-full of suggestions, group processes, and personal growth exercises that build sessions participants will remember!

MAKING HEALTHY CHOICES

Making Healthy Choices, a complete six-session, video-based course on healthy living, encourages people to begin making the choices, large and small, that promote wellness in all areas of their lives. Save $95.00 by purchasing the complete set or select individual sessions.

- ❑ **MAKING HEALTHY CHOICES SET / $474.00**
- ❑ **Healthy Lifestyle / $95.00**
- ❑ **Healthy Eating / $95.00**
- ❑ **Healthy Exercise / $95.00**
- ❑ **Healthy Stress / $95.00**
- ❑ **Healthy Relationships / $95.00**
- ❑ **Healthy Change / $95.00**

MANAGING JOB STRESS

Managing Job Stress, a comprehensive six-session stress management course, takes aim at a universal problem: work-related stress. Each session emphasizes positive responses to the challenges of on-the-job stress. Save $95.00 by purchasing the entire set or select individual sessions.

- ❑ **MANAGING JOB STRESS SET / $474.00**
- ❑ **Handling Workplace Pressure / $95.00**
- ❑ **Clarifying Roles and Expectations / $95.00**
- ❑ **Controlling the Workload / $95.00**
- ❑ **Managing People Pressures / $95.00**
- ❑ **Surviving the Changing Workplace / $95.00**
- ❑ **Balancing Work and Home / $95.00**

MANAGE IT!

Manage It! is an innovative six-part video-based series that helps participants develop management skills for handling stress. Participants learn new coping skills and practice a relaxation technique for immediate on-the-spot stress relief. Save $95.00 by purchasing the entire set or select individual sessions.

- ❑ **MANAGE IT! SET / $474.00**
- ❑ **Stress Traps / $95.00**
- ❑ **Stress Overload / $95.00**
- ❑ **Interpersonal Conflict / $95.00**
- ❑ **Addictive Patterns / $95.00**
- ❑ **Job Stress / $95.00**
- ❑ **Survival Skills / $95.00**

To order, call toll free   (800) 247-6789

WORKSHOPS-IN-A-BOOK

Workshops-in-a-book are developed to be used as a classroom text, discussion guide, and participant workbook; a professional resource for both novice and experienced trainers; a personal journey for individuals; all in an easy-to-understand, user-friendly format.

KICKING YOUR STRESS HABITS:
A Do-it-yourself Guide for Coping with Stress
Donald A. Tubesing, PhD

Over a quarter of a million people have found ways to deal with their everyday stress by using **Kicking Your Stress Habits**. This workshop-in-a-book actively involves the reader in assessing stressful patterns and developing more effective coping strategies with helpful "Stop and Reflect" sections in each chapter.

The 10-step planning process and 20 skills for managing stress make **Kicking Your Stress Habits** an ideal text for stress management classes in many different settings, from hospitals to universities.

❏ **Kicking Your Stress Habits / $14.95**

SEEKING YOUR HEALTHY BALANCE:
A Do-it-yourself Guide to Whole Person Well-being
Donald A. Tubesing, PhD and Nancy Loving Tubesing, EdD

Where can people find the time and energy to "do it all" without sacrificing health and well-being? **Seeking Your Healthy Balance** helps readers discover how to develop a more balanced life-style by learning effective ways to juggle work, self, and others; by clarifying self-care options; and by discovering and setting their own personal priorities.

Seeking Your Healthy Balance asks the questions that help readers find their own answers.

❏ **Seeking Your Healthy Balance / $14.95**

To order, call toll free   (800) 247-6789

WELLNESS ACTIVITIES FOR YOUTH
Volumes 1 & 2
Sandy Queen

Each volume of **Wellness Activities for Youth** provides 36 complete classroom activities that help leaders teach children and teenagers about wellness with a whole person approach and an emphasis on FUN.

The concepts include:

- values
- stress and coping
- self-esteem
- personal well-being
- social wellness

❏ **Wellness Activities for Youth Volume 1 & 2 / $19.95 each**

WORKSHEET MASTERS
Complete packages of (8 1/2" x 11") photocopy masters are available for each volume of **Wellness Activities for Youth**. Use the masters to conveniently duplicate handouts for each participant.

❏ **Worksheet Masters / $9.95 per volume**

WHAT DO YOU DO WITH A CHILD LIKE THIS?
L. Tobin

What Do You Do With A Child Like This? takes readers on a journey inside the world of troubled children, inviting empathy, then presenting a variety of proven techniques for helping these children to make the behavior changes that will bring them happier lives. This unique book, filled with innovative and practical tools for teachers, psychologists, and parents has been praised by educators for its sensitivity to the pain of troubled kids.

❏ **What Do You Do With A Child Like This? / $14.95**

To order, call toll free   (800) 247-6789

About Whole Person Associates

At Whole Person Associates, we're 100% committed to providing stress and wellness materials that involve participants and provide a "whole person" focus—body, mind, spirit, and relationships.

That's our mission and it's very important to us—but it doesn't tell the whole story. Behind the products in our catalog is a company full of people—and *that's* what really makes us who we are.

ABOUT THE OWNERS
Whole Person Associates was created by the vision of two people: Donald A. Tubesing, PhD, and Nancy Loving Tubesing, EdD. Since way back in 1970, Don and Nancy have been active in the stress management/wellness promotion movement—consulting, leading seminars, writing, and publishing. Most of our early products were the result of their creativity and expertise.

Living proof that you can "stay evergreen," Don and Nancy remain the driving force behind the company and are still very active in developing new products that touch people's lives.

ABOUT THE COMPANY
Whole Person Associates was "born" in Duluth, Minnesota, and we remain committed to our lovely city on the shore of Lake Superior. All of our operations are here, which makes communication between departments much easier! We've grown since our beginnings, but at a steady pace—we're interested in sustainable growth that allows us to keep our down-to-earth orientation.

We put the same high quality into every product we offer, translating the best of current research into practical, accessible, easy-to-use materials. In this way we can create the best possible resources to help our customers teach about stress management and wellness promotion.

We also strive to treat our customers as we would like to be treated. If we fall short of our goals in any way, please let us know.

ABOUT OUR EMPLOYEES
Speaking of down-to-earth, that's a requirement for each and every one of our employees. We're all product consultants, which means that anyone who answers the phone can probably answer your questions (if they can't, they'll find someone who can.)

We focus on helping you find the products that fit your needs. And we've found that the best way to accomplish that is by hiring friendly and resourceful people.

ABOUT OUR ASSOCIATES

Who are the "associates" in Whole Person Associates? They're the trainers, authors, musicians, and others who have developed much of the material you see on these pages. We're always on the lookout for high-quality products that reflect our "whole person" philosophy and fill a need for our customers.

Most of our products were developed by experts who are at the top of their fields, and we're very proud to be associated with them.

ABOUT OUR CUSTOMERS

Finally, we wouldn't have a reason to exist without you, our customers. We've met some of you, and we've talked to many more of you on the phone. We are always aware that without you, there would be no Whole Person Associates.

That's why we'd love to hear from you! Let us know what you think of our products—how you use them in your work, what additional products you'd like to see, and what shortcomings you've noted. Write us or call on our toll-free line. We look forward to hearing from you!